From Wrags To Ritches

Sharon Levette Coleman

authorHOUSE®

AuthorHouse™
1663 Liberty Drive
Bloomington, IN 47403
www.authorhouse.com
Phone: 1 (800) 839-8640

Published by AuthorHouse 04/21/2018

ISBN: 978-1-4259-9453-2 (sc)

Print information available on the last page.

CONTENTS

PREFACE

    First, I would like to give honor and thanks to God for using me as a vessel, to tell the truth, the whole truth and nothing but the truth; and for giving me the motivation, endurance, and spiritual arm to take upon the challenge and responsibility of completing this true story.

    Secondly, I want to thank mom for repenting and having that talk with God, and even more importantly for writing through me. I thank her for coming to me in the rain and near the water and for the signs that she shared with all of us.

    To my immediate family, husband, son and two daughters, thanks for listening and praying with me and for believing that I would come through it a better person.

    To my siblings, thanks for allowing me to openly discuss all the painful things that we experience while growing into who we are today. Thanks for sharing memories both good and bad. Thanks for trusting in that very force of God that great-grandmother beat in us for healing throughout our entire family.

THE PENCIL TURNED

As I started to write the story of my life, my pencil turned. I stopped writing about myself and started to write about my mother. I sat early in the morning with papers scattered all over my luxury bed, in my two-story home writing and gathering information about my family. My two daughters were upstairs sleeping and resting in their bedrooms. My husband was at work in Dallas, and I was off work for the day. It was a beautiful day to be writing because it was raining hard outside. I grabbed my writing pin, gathered my notepads and prepared a hot cup of tea, crawled in my bed and began to write. As I started to write the story, there were pieces that weren't quite coming together. I wanted to write about the beautiful life I was living. Instead, I began writing about the dangerous traps mom had fallen into. I wanted to share how good it felt to travel the world and see places I never imagine visiting. I wanted to share how beautiful the oceans, rivers, and lakes were but instead, I began reflecting upon my childhood memories. I needed help. As the tears began to stream down my face, I realized that some of the reasons my life was rich, were because of the struggles my parents had experienced.

I contemplated sharing my mother's story of struggles because some of them were embarrassing, and I didn't want to embarrass her, and certainly, I didn't want to embarrass myself. I had worked hard to avoid the dysfunctional lifestyle my mother had lived.

It was never my intent to degrade my family accomplishments, but there were many deadly secrets, rumors and painful childhood memories that were still reoccurring and hurting our families. I rather kept the rags a secret, because the rags were raggedy. I was searching deeply for the riches, not the material riches but the riches that would heal broken hearts and fill voids. I was searching for ways to stop the dysfunctional cycles and bad behavioral from reoccurring to our innocent children. I was searching for ways to help others heal, but I realized that I had to heal first.

As I began to let my mind go back to those days, it was true that, I lied to myself and fantasied that the shotgun houses we lived in were beautiful homes. I had covered up the memories of mom once being a junky to alcohol and drugs. I wanted to go straight to the riches and skip over the rags, but it was the rags that got me to the riches. I felt mom's spirit as I pondered how to write the truth. I could hear her say, "It's okay you can tell it, but if you tell it, you must tell the truth, the whole truth and nothing but the truth or don't you tell it." She said, "The story must heal the land!" "Heal the land" she repeated. I asked Mom, "How does the story heal the land?" She said, "By telling the truth." The pencil turned, I stopped writing about me and started writing about her.

"In Honor of Mother... My Friend"
Ethel Lee Coleman
December 2, 1939 - November 29, 2003

SHARING CHILDHOOD MEMORIES

I called my siblings and told them I was writing a story about our family; they were all excited. As I began to talk to my siblings, relatives, and others involved, I had no idea of the graveyards I was about to physically walk and revisit mentally. We all expressed some of our pain, as we openly talked about our parent's struggles and how we had been affected by them. I began to remember - so much. We talked about those childhood memories I never cared to remember. I had buried them inside of me.

My sister offered to take me for a ride to show me some of the places we once lived. I called the girls nanny to watch them for a while, gathered my things, jumped in my truck and went to pick her up. When I arrived at my florist shop, she got in the truck and off we went. As we drove through the City of Memphis, Tennessee revisiting the areas the story took place, we discussed the years it took place, which were between 1939 and 2006. We visited the schools, cafe's, dope houses, orphanage homes, boarded up apartments, mental institutions, rooming and shotgun houses, we once lived in. We visited the hotels, and vacant mechanic shops that we had left many bad memories inside. We visited the sidewalks our furniture had been put out on, and the grave yards we walk through to get to school.

I found myself at ease writing the story once I felt mom would be okay with it. I felt anointed by God and appointed by Mom to tell the story. During my writing, I focused on telling the truth. I kept reminding myself, to tell the truth, the whole truth and nothing but the truth. I repeated mom's words, "The story must help to heal the land."

I became frightened, as my sister continued to drive to some of the places. I asked my sister to take me to the graveyard we walked through to get to school when we were 5, 7, 8 and 9-year-old, children. She drove up and let me out. There were graves on each side. I walked and walked, and then I ran, which seemed like for hours. I wanted to feel how it felt to walk through the graveyards as children, only to be told by the principal once we arrived school, that we had to go back home to get a note.

As we revisited some of the neighborhoods we once lived in, I wondered how I made it through. I was scared, and I didn't feel safe. The thought of once living in some of the places made me shiver, but when I was a child, I gave it very little thought. As my sister continued to drive and explain the stories to me, I began to remember some harsh things that happen to our family. I felt my entire family's pain, and tears dropped from my eyes.

THEY REMIND ME OF US

My sister and I drove up to the apartments where my aunt once lived, on Patton Street. The memories of sitting and waiting on the sidewalk for mom for hours got clearer. Mom never showed up, but auntie came for us and kept us for several weeks. Tears continued to flow down my eyes as I thought about how I worried wondering where my mom could have been.

Outside there stood four children that reminded me of us. There were two girls and two boys. One little girl looked like Jackie, my oldest sister. The little girl, was slim with yellow skin, dark brown hair, brown-eyes with her hair all over her head; she appeared to be baby-sitting the other children. One little boy looked like Craig, my oldest brother. He was slim, tall, light caramel brown skin, deep dark brown eyes, quiet, and off to himself. The other little boy looked like my older but youngest brother, Oliviodale. He had dark brown skin, he was short, stocky frame, with jet black eyes. He wore a hood that covered his head and some baggy jeans. He looked like he was ready to fight the first person that said something out of line to him. The other little girl reminded me of myself, Sharon, the youngest of the four siblings. She had caramel peanut butter skin, dark to light brown eyes, and sandy brown hair - very sassy, aggressive and assertive. She had a personality that expressed, confidence. They were all outside in their dusty, worn clothes, with their shoes untied and coats un-button. The screen doors to the apartments were swinging open and close. The garbage cans were running over with trash, and papers were scattered all over the yards. The neighborhood was heavily blighted.

The woman that appeared to be their mother was on her way upstairs to another apartment. She looked like she hadn't been sleeping. The youngest little girl said to me, "What do you want lady?" I said to the little girl, "I used to live here, and I'm writing a true story about my family life, and I would like to take a picture of the apartments." She said lady, "Take our picture." She called the boys from upstairs and said, "Come on, let's take a picture for the woman." The two boys ran downstairs, and they all posed for the picture. The oldest girl had gone into the apartment. After taking the picture, I returned to my truck; the youngest girl said, "Hey lady, are you coming back?" I said yes, "I'll be back." The bad memories I had covered up as good were getting clearer; tears started to roll down my face again. I opened the truck door to get in, and the little girl yelled, "Hey lady, are you sure you're coming back?" Again, I said, "Yes I'm sure - I'll be back." Her question brought back memories of how I felt when I was a little girl and mom was gone. She asked again and again, "You're sure you're coming back lady - are you sure you're coming back?" I kept repeating, "I'm coming back!" They were four children that reminded me of how meek, humble and innocent we were as children. They reminded me of how our rags were our riches. Though their environment looked unhealthy and unsafe, they didn't appear to be unhappy or worried. In my head, I understood her to say, "Hey lady, why are you here?" "You've got on your nice clothes and driving a new truck, what are you going to do - go call the people on us? Are you going to embarrass us, or are you going to tell the social workers to come take us from our momma?" I flashed back to memories of how I once felt, when we waited on mom for long hours. I was afraid that we would be taken by the social workers that often visit the neighborhood, checking on women that received welfare and food stamps. I knew if the social workers knew mom was leaving us at home alone for days at a time we would be taken away.

As we drove off, I looked out of my window at the children and shook my head knowing that I wouldn't do anything to hurt those children. I told my sister, I would never send a social worker back for those children, because they didn't appear unhappy, their mother did. I left there with a desire to help families in their environment. I told my sister that I pray one day this world will find help for mother's that are struggling like that mother, because she reminded me of mom. Our mother was a beautiful lady that had fallen into a trap after she and dad separated. She made some bad decisions and couldn't find the resources she needed to get out of the trap; she had fallen into. The resources of giving her food stamps, welfare and putting her in a low subsidizing apartment didn't help her mindset. She adjusted to living in an environment surrounded by poverty.

EXPRESSIONS OF RELIEF

I looked at my sister and saw the expression of relief on her face as we continued to discuss our childhood memories openly. I could feel her releasing some of the pressure she had held inside for so long. She had dealt with the family childhood memories alone for many years, and now I was grown I was ready to face the truth and deal with the ones I had buried. At an early age, my sister had the responsibility of an adult, and sometimes that resulted in her being taken advantage of by dirty men. I was the youngest of the four children; my siblings protected me from as much pain and abuse as they could. They didn't have a clue that I too had experienced some ugly things by some of those same dirty old men that touched my sister.

IN LOVE BUT MARRIED
TO YOUNG

I considered that mom and dad being so young had a lot to do with the bad decisions that they made. The first bad decision was when mom and dad dropped out of school. They were young. Mom was 16 and dad was 18. They were pregnant with their first child, but mom miscarried the baby in a little shack in Darling, Mississippi.

They married and ran away from Darling, to Memphis, Tennessee, hoping to find a better lifestyle. Mom was raised by her grandmother Ella Perkins; her mother left her at the age of 4. Ella Perkins was a single-parent. She never married. She was a mean Christian woman and a strict great-grandparent. Great-grandmother, mother, died when she was 12, and her father was found dead in the woods shortly afterwards. He was an alcoholic. Great-grandmother was left responsible for raising her siblings and her three children. None of them were raised with their father's in their lives. She was a single parent.

My father was raised by both of his parents. His father was a pastor; he prayed over cloth that were used to heal people. He was a righteous man. His mother was humble, sweet and faithful. Grandmother was dedicated to her family. Papa and grandmother stayed married until death separated them. I remembered her praying on her dying bed, that her children and grandchildren would get to know God and live a righteous life. Papa died before I was old enough to remember but I recall grandmother funeral. I cried because I knew I would miss her, but it also hurt to see my daddy sad.

Dad was described as a tall, brown skin, dark hair, black eyes, handsome, well-groomed, friendly, respectful, introverted young man. He left Darling, Mississippi to come to Memphis, Tennessee to start a life with his wife in 1955. He wanted to escape poverty and the lack of opportunity for education in the South. He wanted to find work. The only jobs Darling, Mississippi had to offer a black man was farming, and there wasn't much of that going on. He had three siblings, two older sisters, and one older brother. Dad had a loving relationship with his father and mother and set out to have a loving relationship with his wife. He often told us the story about his father and the prayer cloth used to heal and save people. It amazed me to know that my grandfather was a Pastor that many people looked up to. He was a Pastor that many honored for the work he did in his community, family, and church.

Mom was a beautiful young girl, best described as, medium height 5'5", yellow skin, wavy hair, hazel brown eyes, beautiful smile, with a Coca-Cola bottle shape. She was friendly with a beautiful personality. She left Darling, Mississippi, to escape the lifestyle of poverty hoping she would begin a life with her young teenage husband and build a happy future. She wanted to be love and overcome the hurt she had experienced as a young girl raised without her mother and father. Her desire and dreams were to finish school and become successful. She often told us the story of how she missed her mother. She didn't have much to say about her father because she said, she never got to know him.

Mom had two siblings, a younger sister, and younger brother. Her mother left them with great-grandmother, Ella Perkins. My mother never bonded with her mother or father. I learned that her father was a handsome brown-skinned man. He had nine children, by several different women. It was said that he drank a lot and liked to fight.

Grandmother left Darling, Mississippi to get away from him. She moved to St. Louis where she found a job and sent money back to Darling, Mississippi for them. She would periodically visit them, but she never moved them to St. Louis, because her man had three children and didn't want more children. I called him Uncle James instead of Grandpa James. When he and grandma visited Mississippi, they would take us for hamburgers.

LOW-INCOME NEIGHBORHOODS

When mom and dad moved to Memphis in 1955, they moved to a low-income neighborhood called Washington Bottom. They were excited to begin a new life other than that of Darling, Mississippi. Their rent was based on their income. Daddy was the only one working. Dad said, after living there for a while he and mom moved, he said he didn't like the environment. They moved to Foot Homes Apartments, another low-income housing projects. Dad said, he wasn't pleased with that environment either, but mom didn't want to move, so he prayed for the best and stayed.

Mom became pregnant with their second child she was born in 1957, they named her Jackie Cole. One year later, Mom became pregnant with their third child he was born in 1958, they named him Craig Cole. Dad drove a truck for a living and traveled from city to city. The rumor was mom was having an affair with a man while dad was on the road, and Mom got pregnant with their fourth child, he was born in 1959. They named him Oliviodale Cole. She went to St. Louis to birth him; she told her brother she was going to leave him there at the hospital. Her brother asked her, why? She wouldn't answer. He told her if she did, he would adopt him, but instead, she brought him back to Memphis. Then mom became pregnant with me and I was born in 1961, they name me Sharon Cole. Mom was pregnant every year for six years. She was pregnant with twins, but they died. Mom said, she was on a ladder when I was about to put my hands in the fan, she jumped to prevent me from hurting myself, and she miscarried the twins.

Mom became bored with being a housewife. She wanted to go to school and find herself a good job, but that didn't happen. She started choosing the wrong people as her friends. Dad told her he didn't think it was a good idea making friends with the people and suggested she not trust the neighbors, but she started arguments with dad so that she could get out the house. Dad said, mom began to complain about being bored and tired of taking care of children all day, every-day. Mom hadn't considered the consequences of being married at a young age nor had she considered the consequences of having children at a very young age.

Mom had never traded her body for money, used drugs, smoked, stole, or drank alcohol, however; the neighborhood friends she met were stealing, selling, using drugs and prostituting themselves. Mom was a young southern girl, that didn't have her parents in her life to guide her, she didn't know much about life. When dad got in from work, mom would start arguments and fights, so she could go hang out with her friends. Next mom started withdrawing the little money dad had from his account to purchase drugs. Dad said, he gave her money a few times, he said: "I couldn't continue to support her habits, because I realized I wasn't helping her, I was hurting her." He said, when he didn't give mom money to support her habit, she got angry and out of control, but he wasn't going to fight her, because he wasn't raised to hit a woman. Dad said, "I would often leave the house and take a walk until she settled down."

Many of the people that I encountered while doing my research, told me stories of how beautiful she was. They talked about her bubbling personality and happy smile. They shared stories of how she could charm and lure most people in with her personality. Unfortunately, the drugs affected that, and dad and mom separated shortly after their fifth child was born. Mom was 24 and dad was 26 when they separated. Dad moved back to Chicago, and mom stayed in Memphis.

THE STRUGGLES OF
A SINGLE PARENT

Mom began her life as a single parent with four children, while dad was in Chicago trying to start his life over. He visited Memphis occasionally, and brought money for us. He couldn't mail it because mom moved so often. Life got harder for mom once dad left, she started making her income like her friends in the neighborhood. She started hanging out with people that were stealing, selling drugs, forging checks and writing illegal prescriptions for a window pane, codeine, and antidepressants.

She began moving from place to place. We lived in low-income neighborhoods, because mom didn't have a job. Mom depended on government assistance. The apartments we lived in were small. Some of the apartments around ours were boarded up because they were vacant.

The drugs began to control mom's mind; she stayed out in the streets days at a time. It didn't matter how long mom would be gone, all four of us waited together until she showed up. We were subjected to our surroundings, and our surroundings weren't good. Being so young we didn't know what to appreciate, so we appreciated whatever was offered to us, which wasn't much. Sometimes we played in the empty apartments and other times we climbed trees and billboards. We found things to do to stay busy.

We had lived forty different places by the time I was 6 years-old okay I maybe exaggerating, but close to it. A couple of occasions, my aunt was forced to take us in. Auntie had eight children of her own and didn't have room for four more children. She stayed in the "hood," but she dressed her house up by putting pretty paint on the outside of it. She was married and living a lifestyle that most people called a stable life. She prepared her children's breakfast and made their lunches to take to school.

She and her husband fought, but auntie hid the bruises from everybody. Mom knew when her sister had gotten into a fight, because when she asked her what was wrong, she wouldn't answer. Instead, she looked at the ground with tears in her eyes. Mom rarely visited, but when she walked into the house, he got quiet. Mom threatened him and told him, if he continued to put his hands on her sister, she would cut his fingers off. Mom meant what she said. She didn't mind fighting. He got the message. Mom and her sister loved one another, but they had their differences. They didn't communicate so they never bonded. Mom and her brother both drank and suppressed their pain of not having a relationship with their parents. Auntie didn't drink to get drunk; she said she drank to relax. Auntie said she pushed herself on grandmother to have a relationship with her. Mom left her sister and brother in Darling with their grandmother, Ella Perkins. Her brother and sister were sad because mom was the oldest, and they feared being stuck. Mom promised she would come back for them, but that didn't happen. They eventually left. Auntie moved to Memphis; she said she wanted to be near her sister, and Uncle Percy moved to St. Louis where grandmother and her husband James lived. James and Uncle Percy never got alone. Grandmother would sneak him money when he needed it. She didn't want her husband James to know.

I remembered the time mom left all four of us in the apartments alone; she was in jail - we didn't know where to go. Dad was in Chicago, and we didn't have anyone to call but our auntie, we were young. Our auntie came to our rescue again. She kept us again for several weeks until my dad came for us and took us to our great-grandmother's house. Like always auntie didn't have much food to share because she had a large family, but she stretched what she had, and we appreciated her for that.

RUMORS OF
PATERNITY ISSUES

For a long time, we heard the rumors in great-grandmother's house about my youngest brother and me not being my dad's biological children. It was at age 33, that our cousin brought the rumor back up. He asked my brother something about his real dad.

My brother replied, "What do you mean about my real dad?" My cousin went on to say, "Your dad is Mr. Harry." My brother was angry with mom for a year and avoided speaking to her. I asked my brother if he remembered the rumors we heard when we were little kids. He said, "No", but I know he remembered because I did. He buried those memories, like many other rumors we had buried about our childhood life. He said he was angry that mom hadn't talked to him about the rumor. We had a long talk that night. I suggested he talked to mom about the rumor. One day he went over, and asked mom was the rumor true. She never said yes. She said, she did what she had to do to get money. She admitted she was young and made some bad decisions. She still didn't admit, that the man was my brother's dad. She told him the only dad he had was Henry. I told my brother dad was the only man that rescued us in the time of need, and the man shouldn't matter because regardless; if the rumors were true the man didn't deserve any recognition as our father. He had never supported us.

I refreshed my brother's memory about the time mom, he and I went to a store called, Sears. I recalled mom going to get money from the man. Mom didn't have a car; I recalled her catching a cab to get there. When we arrived he would say, he didn't have the money, or he would tell her to come back later; however, she didn't have the money to go back later, because we had ridden in a cab to get there. I remembered being sad that mom had to ask him for help only for him to say no.

I overheard great-grandmother, grandmother and auntie say dad wasn't my father, and that man, we visited at Sears was my daddy too. I was young and didn't care about the rumors they spread. I never cared whether he was my father or not. I never wanted to know the man, because he had never provided shelter or food for my family. I knew only one man as my father. I told my brother, I would never allow someone that never cared to claim me, make me bitter. All I wanted was to know the truth, so that I could face it and continue to write my story, but the outcome wouldn't make a difference at this stage in my life.

There were many rumors going around, and some of them were just lies, but I wanted to learn the truth. I had it in my head that mom and dad separated after I was born, but my sister, Jackie said that mom and dad separated after my oldest brother Craig was born. If the rumor were true, that would mean since I was born after Oliviodale it would be a possibility that Mr. Harry was my father. I continued typing, shocked at my findings, but I never stopped writing.

I contacted the guy's brother and asked him some questions hoping to find more truth. He said he knew my mother and his brother were messing around when my brother was conceived, but he was sure that they weren't messing around when I was born. I thought to myself; I may be the milk man's baby. In so many words, I wouldn't know who my dad was if I got caught up in everyone's rumors. So, I chose to be grateful to have a man in my life that I had called dad from the day I was born and refused to let the possibility affect me in a negative way. After all, my dad never made a difference in any of his children. I continue to write the story. The more I uncovered the memories, the more I could feel the pain of my family. I cried a lot during my writing of my mother's story, because the truth hurt, but the more I wrote, the more I could feel myself healing from the bad memories.

Dad had two girls, and two boys by my mother, and later had two girls by another lady, after he and mom divorced.

WE NEED OUR DADDY
EVIL STEPMOTHER

Judy was our stepmother; she was a pretty lady. She and Dad had two daughters together. At first, I was angry that dad had another woman in his life, because we needed him. I wasn't ready to share my father with anyone else. However, I thought maybe she would love us. I became excited at first, until we visit our dad, and learn she was an evil, mean woman. She was jealous that my hair was long and curly and pressed it with cooking lard. She beat my baby brother Oliviodale, because he went in the refrigerator to find food to eat, she threaten Craig to tell dad he was misbehaving, and she allowed Jackie to smoke cigarettes, only to have something to threaten her with. She made it clear that we weren't her responsibility and she wasn't going to take care of us. She did whatever she could to make dad take us back to our great-grandmother house. Dad told her he wasn't going to make a difference between the two families and if she couldn't help him with us, she could leave. That didn't stop her from being mean to us. I was angry when dad would take us back to great-grandmother house, because all kind of bad things were happening to us. I was young and didn't know how to express my feelings, but I wanted badly to tell him, I hated him for letting that lady come between us. He knew mom was sick. How could he let this happen to us?

My sister told me that our mean stepmother had attempted to pour lye in dad's face. She told me something that happened that I didn't remember. My sister told me the lady was practicing sorcery. I do remember there were times she would sprinkle salt around the door before daddy came in. She did everything to keep daddy all to herself and practicing witchcraft was something she felt would keep them together. My sister said, "One night, daddy was coming in from work, she had placed the pot of lye over the door." My sister said, she dared her to say something. She dared all of us, but my sister said, she still ran to the window and started to scream so that dad wouldn't open the door. Daddy heard her tell him not to open the door. He didn't. Instead, he came in the back door and learned that night that we hadn't been lying about her; she was mean and cruel to us. After a few more altercations with her, they divorced. I was happy that he did.

I remembered dad combing my hair, because he didn't have help. I didn't care how it looked I appreciated him for trying. I forgave him once he divorced that lady. I love him more today than ever. The more I continued to write the story the more I loved both of my parents regardless of how their struggles affected me. I must be honest the things I was learning hurt, and I could have easily chosen to carry the hatred in my hearts forever, but the more I went back I found that dysfunctional behavior transfers all the way back from slavery. If we think about the things our ancestors experienced, I'm sure once they became free they all had poor childhood memories too. I looked at my parent's lives, and began to understand that they were much closer to slavery than I was. They didn't have as much freedom or opportunities as we have today. I began to feel empathy for them.

Had I not decided to search for the truth of my family life I would have thought mom and dad had abandoned me, but that wasn't true. Mom was sick with a habit that she couldn't break, and leaving us for dad to come for us may have been best. Unfortunately, dad was dealing with different women that were selfish and didn't want us around. I closed my eyes and wandered off thinking about the times we were left on the streets in abandoned apartments. I'm sure mom wouldn't have left us if she could have controlled that killer addiction to drugs and alcohol. I appreciated dad for coming for us, though I didn't appreciate him dropping us off at great-grandma house. They both were struggling trying to get themselves together, and we were affected by it.

I often asked myself what we would have done without his love. Dad didn't have a favorite, and if he did, we never knew which child was his favorite - he loved us all. Though there had been rumors that there were three of dad's children in question, my father never questioned my mother or his second wife, about any of us. He loved us all the same.

GREAT-GRANDMOTHER HOUSE

Dad said he was forced to take us to great grandma house at times, because he didn't have help. I didn't like going to Mississippi, because great grandma was strict. My sister pressed my hair and made me look pretty for school. Our great-grandmother poured water in my head because she said we couldn't wear our hair pressed. She would plat my hair and used strings from the blanket to put at the end of my plats. I was angry with her, however; I would keep quiet and pray that mom would soon return to us. The same God mom told us about was the same God I asked to send my parents to me. I must be honest; I questioned if God was real.

We picked cotton for hours and sometimes made $2.00 each for the entire day. We were excited to earn money, but once we got home great-grandmother would take our money, she said we had to save it. After saving our money for months, great-grandmother would take us into town to the secondhand store, and she would make us purchase used clothes. I was angry, because I felt I had earned money and I should have been able to purchase toys to play with. Our father sent her money every month to help pay for shelter, food, and clothes for us, but she said, we had to buy more clothes.

In Mississippi, we didn't have in door toilets. Great-grandmother had an outdoor outhouse. The outhouse was a little wood shack in the backyard, and sometimes the snakes would be in the feces moving around. It was always scary to use the outhouse. There were many times I rushed to use the outhouse, and I ended up peeing on myself because I feared a snake moving around. Great-grandmother had a slope jar in her bedroom for her personal use. We couldn't use her slope jar unless it was an emergency and the emergency had to be in the middle of the night. My brother, Olivodale would have an emergency occasionally, because he had a weak bladder. Great-grandmother whipped him for using it regardless of his emergency. She said he was lazy.

STOP TALKING
ABOUT MY MOMMA

Day in and day out I prayed for mom and dad to come for us because I didn't like living with great-grandmother. She made the boys kill chickens for dinner. I wasn't going to help kill chickens. Every time she said, it was time to kill them I found something to do. I watched my brothers catch them from out the windows; she would break their necks and hang them upside down for the blood to drain. After the blood had drained, she cleaned them and cooked them for our dinner. It was horrible to witness, and when she put the dead chicken on my plate, I didn't eat it. I waited for her to leave the kitchen and I empty my plate in the garbage, sometimes I hid it under the couch.

I remembered a big snake being in her back yard. I was screaming for help. She came out with a garden tool, and she chopped the snake's head off with a garden tool. She put the snake in the garbage can and started a fire. The snake didn't stop moving until the sun went down.

I called great-grandmother a hypocrite because she bragged to her church members about us and said sweet things about us in front of them, but when we were alone with her, she acted totally different. She always told us stories about the bad things mom got herself into. When we did something, she wasn't pleased with she told us we were going to be just like our mother. No good for nothing. I was sassy; I told her I wanted to be like my mother. I knew of good things about my mother. We loved our mom regardless of what abuse she was putting herself through - we loved that woman. I asked great-grandmother to please stop talking about my mother. She would tell me to shut up. Great-grandmother found reasons to beat us. I'm sure there were sometimes we needed a whipping, but to beat us for something our mom had done wasn't fair.

Jackie and Craig would run away from the house at times. Oliviodale and I would just listen to great-grandma fuss. We would laugh and make jokes while she complained. I said, what was on my mind, and when great-grandmother talked bad about mom, I got behind the door and threw "F-U" signs at her. I hated living with her, and I let her know every opportunity I got that I wanted my momma and I wanted my daddy. There was nothing anyone could tell me to stop me from loving my parents. We were all happy when mom got out of jail and came for us.

We gathered our things and returned to Memphis.

THE WRONG FRIENDS
LED TO DRUGS

The company mom was hanging with were disgusting. They did anything to get money. The women played games on the men. They often promised the men sex knowing they were lying and they put pills in the men drinks, got them high and took their money. Mom met this guy named Zack; he sold drugs. He owned a small neighborhood sundry. He was known in the "hood" as a "big baller." Mom was attracted to him because he was popular, and he was powerful. All the women in the neighborhood liked him. He lured mom in with his charm.

Zack liked mom because she was innocent, and she was the new girl on the block. He had already started mom to indulging in drinking alcohol and smoking marijuana. He gave her as much marijuana as she wanted because he was the dope man. All she had to do was hangout with him. Mom said one night she was drinking and smoking marijuana with Zack, and he put some cocaine in the marijuana. She said, before she knew it she was asking for more. Soon cocaine became a recreational drug for her, and next, he introduced her to heroin. She said she had fallen into another trap that she couldn't find her way out of. She said all hell broke loose.

Once Zack got mom hooked on the drugs he became controlling. Mom was friendly to both men and women. If Zack caught mom flirting they would get into an argument. One evening Mom and Zack had finished using heroin, they got into an argument about mom flirting with another guy in the neighborhood. Mom cussed him, and he cussed her until the argument escalated into a fight. They began to fight dangerously. Mom was a small girl, he stomped, beat, and kicked her until he broke her ribs. Her face was busted up, and she was bleeding. Mom was taken to the hospital by one of the guys in the neighborhood. We stayed at neighbor's houses up the streets until mom returned. It was a week later. She didn't look good. We had to take care of her until she got better. It hurt seeing mom lying in bed beaten. Dad or great-grandmother didn't know mom was involved in a domestic violent relationship, and we didn't tell him, because we wanted to stay with mom. We were certain that if dad knew he would have come back to get us. We promised mom not to tell. Mom wanted us to stay.

WE WITNESSED DEATH

We walked to Kansas Elementary School every morning. Most of the times we waited for the trains to move and other times we raced across the tracks trying to beat the trains to avoid being late for school. It was dangerous! One day we all witnessed a little boy dying. He was running across the tracks trying to beat the trains; he was cut in half. There was blood everywhere. Half of the little boy's body was on one side of the train, and the other half was on the other side. We were frightened, and it was scary to see the little boy's guts hanging onto the train. He died instantly. We rushed home, told mom what happened to the little boy, and she said to be careful. We still had to cross the rail road tracks every morning to get to school, because there was no other way around it. Olivodale said he never forget that day. I couldn't remember seeing the little boy guts, but I do remember him getting hit by the train and all the blood on the tracks.

I asked my sister why mom always accused her of messing around with her men. My sister said mom men were dirty. She told me how Zack had shown her his penis a couple of times. She told me how he approached her sexually. She told him she would tell mom if he continued, but he threatened to tell mom she had approached him. My sister was scared mom wouldn't believe her, and she felt mom would take his side, so she never said anything to mom about what he was doing. Mom needed him to continue supplying her habit. She wouldn't listen to Jackie. After mom healed from her ribs being broken, she left Zack because of his abusive ways. She met a man named Fred. Fred offered us to stay with him.

She moved around the corner on Walker and LaClede with Fred in another sat of low-income apartments. Fred was tall, fair skin, straight hair, quiet, but sneaky and he moved about slowly. He used the syrup to get high. He didn't argue or fight with mom, but he shot heroin, and wrote illegal prescriptions for pills. Fred hustled and stole mink and leather coats. Mom and Fred stayed on the run from the police, because they were wanted for stealing and writing illegal prescriptions.

Right when we thought things were getting better for mom, she got another eviction notice.

Mom didn't pay the rent, and we had to move again. Mom and Fred were gone that day when the people came and put our things out on the streets. We cried as people came up and took our things. My two brother's bikes were taken by some of the boys in the neighborhood. The boys were bullies. There wasn't anything we could do, we were young, and they were older children. We did what we did often when mom didn't show up, and we were waiting on the sidewalk patiently until she showed up. It had gotten dark outside, the winds were high, and it had begun to rain. We sat there in the rain trying to protect our things. Finally, mom showed up with a guy, he helped mom to get as much of our things as they could, and the rest mom left on the streets.

DAD LEFT AGAIN TO MUCH TROUBLE IN MEMPHIS

Somehow dad found out mom wasn't doing well and moved back to Memphis. We were happy, because we knew we could run to dad when things weren't going well. One-night dad went out to a night club. He was flirting and laughing with this woman. Dad was an occasional social drinker. He didn't hang out and nor did he fight women. Dad said, he was at the nightclub flirting with a woman, when another lady friend approached him with a knife. She tapped him on his shoulder - he turned around into the knife. The knife left a long cut on dad's face. Jackie said when she saw dad he had a bandage on his face. He stayed in Memphis for a few months, but shortly after that happened, he went back to Chicago. He said it was too much trouble in Memphis. He left for Chicago and never came back to live. We were sad little children when dad left.

ON THE MOVE AGAIN

We moved to a house this time on Shoney Street. It was a small three-bedroom house, kitchen, front room, dining room and nice front and back yard. We loved that house. It felt more like a home.

It was the year of 1968. I was 7 years old. I remembered that day clearly because Dr. Martin Luther King Jr. was killed that year. It was a scary evening in Memphis that night. Leaves were flying everywhere, and sirens were going off everywhere. It seemed like the world was coming to an end. One of our most inspirational black men had been assassinated. We were frightened and worried for mom because she wasn't home. I recall doing what big momma taught us to do. I prayed that mom would make it home safely. Soon mom returned home, and we were happy.

I thought we were living large when we move on Shoney. I thought we were rich. I was proud to say we lived in the white house that sat on the hill. It was the first time we had lived in a house with mom; however, we always stayed in the four-story houses with our father. The house was white, with fresh paint on the outside. It sat on a hill all to itself. I was excited because, we had a front yard and a back yard.

We walked to school, and sometimes mom would call us a cab, depending on how late we were.

I sometimes cried when we walked to school because it took so long to get there. I regretted the long walk through the graveyards. After school, we would come home, and if mom weren't there, we would wait on the porch. She would pull up late, and I could tell she had been drinking. We would be hungry by the time she got there. There were times my sister would find ways to get us food. There was a rumor that she was selling her body for money, but I think she was playing games on the dirty old men as mom had done. She would tell us to wait and when she returned she brought us chips and drinks back. My sister was very young, but she managed to watch after us.

IT'S A WHITE CHRISTMAS

We were all young. My sister was 10; my oldest brother was 9, my other youngest brother of the two was 8 and, I was 7. We were all excited about the white Christmas tree. The tree had revolving multi-color lights going around it. Mom had Christmas lights hanging around the windows, wreaths on the doors and the windows. It was very pretty in our little white house. I remembered the carpet being white; it reminded me of snow. We had red apples, pecans and the big peppermint candy cane on the bar. Mom left cookies on the counter; she said the cookies were for Santa. I asked mom a couple of times was Santa our dad. She told me to be a good girl, and I would see. Some of our best moments were spent in that house, we were happy. Mom was occasionally cooking for us, and the house stayed clean. We were all excited about the toys mom had promised we would get for Christmas. I couldn't wait to see what Santa had brought us. I knew mom was going to get me the life-size doll, I asked her for, and I had a strong feeling that daddy would be home for Christmas. Soon Christmas came we opened our gifts and went outside in the snow to play. I didn't get my life size doll or my daddy for Christmas, but I did get skates, a doll, and a bike. I was happy to go out and play with my siblings.

MOM HE TOUCHED ME

Fred was still staying with us, he got drunk one night and put his hand under my dress. He touched me inappropriately. I screamed and yelled for mom. When she came in the room, I told her that Mr. Fred had touched me under my clothes. Mom confronted him. She told me to leave out the room for a minute. I heard her ask him did he try to touch me. He said, "No". Mom threaten to beat him with a baseball bat. He never attempted to touch me again.

One-night mom was in the kitchen cooking. She poured herself a drink. Once she finished, she poured herself another one, and another one and another one. I was young, but I noticed mom personality changing the more she drank the liquor. I asked mom why did she drink so much. She said she was trying to stop, but the habit was hard to break. I remembered her touching my cheeks as she said, "Drinking helps mommy with the buried pain I have locked up inside of me." I remembered her crying as she explained that she didn't have anyone to talk, so she sedated the pain with alcohol. I asked my sister did mom ever tell her she wanted to stop drinking.

She said she couldn't recall, but she recalled telling mom she needed to seek help.

STOLEN STUFF

We remembered Mom and Fred stealing our clothes, because we went with them to different stores. I remembered going to the mink stores, Downtown with them. Mommy taught me to stand in front of the counter and talk to the cashiers while she and Fred stuffed mink coats in the empty garbage cans. They stole racks of minks and leather coats. I remembered us having a closet full of color televisions that they had stolen. We had color televisions when black and white televisions were the only televisions people had in their homes. I thought we were rich, because people didn't have color televisions back then. We had a lot of material stuff, but some of the things I remembered not having was the feeling of being secure, safe and stable. I told my sister though I never felt safe, I never questioned whether mom loved me.

I remembered getting my head busted. We were in the yard on Shoney Street trying to get some peaches off the tree, and a boy threw a bottle at me, and busted my head. He lived in the apartments across the streets from us. The blood ran down my face; I ran into the house to tell mom. She rushed me to the hospital, and they bandaged my head. When we returned, our doors had been kicked in by the F.B.I. They came in and raided our house of the stolen goods, and took Fred to jail. We had to move again. Mom didn't know what to do, because she had no one in the family to turn to, so she did what she would often do, and that was cash a bad check, and move again to another low-income apartment.

CALL GIRLS

Mom had several friends, but Bertha and Melinda Ann were her oldest friends. They were known as the madams of the call girls. Bertha hooked mom and her younger friends up with men. Some of the men were old attorneys and married businessmen that liked getting freaky with young girls. Bertha charged a few dollars for mom and her friends to bring their men to the house. They would pay Bertha and sometimes Melinda for using their houses to rent a room. They often met the guys there and turned tricks with them. Mom and all her friends were very alluring and attractive. Bertha liked women. Jay-Jay worked the streets prostituting. It hurt my heart to hear her tell me how her mother died when she was 12. She said, she didn't have a mother or father in her life, and she prostituted to survive. Sherrie was married, she did her wrong secretly, because her husband was known as the pimp that sold dope. She feared him finding out she was sleeping around with other guys, because if he knew she was messing around, he would beat her like he had done many times before. Jay-Jay told me that Mattie Sue was a freak and she let dog's lick on her, kitty cat. They were all very young pretty girls. They all had something in common, and that was their parents weren't involved in their lives and they had no one to guide them. It was hard to believe that they were using their bodies to make money, but it was true.

A BLOODY MESS

We moved from the little white house on the hill that made me feel good into an apartment in the projects located on Lauderdale and Philsar. It was a one-bedroom apartment where we all slept. Fred was in jail, and mom was back to running the streets getting high, using cocaine and heroin. She left all four of us in the apartment alone again, for days. One day I was driving around the city and decided to drive by the apartments. The closer I got to the apartments the clearer the memories came back. I parked my car and looked at the steps where mom had come home a bloody mess. I sat in my car and began to cry as the memories of what happened to mom returned. She had been beaten badly, her head and lips were busted, and blood was all over her clothes. Mom had taken this guy named Shorty, money, and drugs. When I asked mom about it, she said she needed money to pay the rent for the apartment and a quick fix to calm her nerves. Mom admitted to doing some disgusting things. She said, Shorty caught up with her walking home late that night and asked for his money. Mom said, she didn't have it, so he took her off and beat her. That's when he brought her to the apartments with a gun to her head and made her beat on the door. I recalled the beat on the door. I remembered being excited because mom had been gone for days. We were hoping that the knock on the door was her. As I sat there in front of the apartments, I recalled my sister opening the door. When she opened the door, she began screaming. Shorty threw mom in the house, and she fell into my sister's arms a bloody mess. She looked horrible. My sister was only 10; she didn't want us to see mom, so she rushed into the bathroom to clean her up. Oliviodale ran out the door to catch the man, while Craig stood in the corner twisting his hair and I cried and sucked my two fingers. People were walking by my car looking in.

One lady asked, "Are you okay?" I said yes, just reminiscing. I cranked my car up and left the site sad.

Jackie always dealt with the most tragic matters. She tried her best to shield us from pain by trying to deal with mom's problems. Jackie settled us down, and we finally went to sleep. The memories were getting clearer and clearer. I drove around the back of the apartments and looked at the back door that I once came out of to play. I looked at the tree my brother, and I climbed often. As I drove off, I continue to think about those days.

THEY TURNED OUR LIGHTS OFF

That night mom got up and left. When we awakened, she was gone, and we were worried. There were many questions in our heads. I remembered asking my sister, did that man come back and get mom or did she sneak into the hospital?

My sister didn't answer. I kept asking questions. I said, "Will mommy be gone for a few days or is mommy dead?" Jackie said, the reason she didn't answer was because she didn't know. She said, she was often not able to answer questions, because she didn't have the answers. She said, there were many times she did things for us that our mom and dad should have been there to do. She told me how some of these things affected her as a child. After a few days, Jackie learned that mom had gone to the hospital where the police had come and taken her to jail again, but this time for forgery of bad checks. We were alone in the apartment for days. Jackie got in touch with my aunt, and my aunt, in turn, contacted our dad. We waited alone for days for dad to arrive from Chicago.

The utility people came and turned the lights off for non-payment, but mom had shown my younger brother how to clip the lock and turn the lights back on. Though it was considered stealing utilities my youngest brother Oliviodale went outside with some wire pliers and turned the lights back on.

The utility company finally came and took the meter to prevent us from stealing more utilities. We were hungry during the days we waited for daddy to show up. My sister Jackie, and my oldest brother Craig caught a big cockroach and began to dissect it. My sister put the roach in a skillet, and she began to fry it. She said we were going to eat the roach for dinner. I started crying. I wanted my mommy and daddy. I was hungry, but I didn't want to eat a cockroach. My brother Craig told me to stop crying. He said they were playing. As we sat on the couch and continued to talk about the story, we laugh because we were hungry enough to consider doing it.

WE SURVIVED

Craig told me that Jackie and he left to find some bottles. At that time bottles sold for 5 cents. They went through garbage cans and looked in people's yards to find bottles to sell to get us something to eat. Craig said they found over thirty bottles. They took the bottles to the store and cashed them in for some meal and sugar. My younger brother and I were afraid to stay in the apartment alone, so we went outside and climbed the big oak tree in the front yard. We stayed in the tree until we saw them return. When they returned, we climbed down the tree and went into the apartment. I was happy to see them return.

Jackie cooked us some hot water cornbread mixed with sugar. This is what we ate, and we were happy, because either we ate the cockroach or be happy for the sweet hot water cornbread. Mom had put away toys for us, for Christmas. We were excited about the toys, because we anticipated having a Christmas with her that year, but after waiting so long for her to return, I doubted she would get back in time for Christmas. I remembered peeping in the closet and seeing the life size doll she promised me. Craig remembered seeing the football she had promised him and Oliviodale remembered she had got him several things. He said he saw batman, car, horses, long rangers and clothes. Jackie said there wasn't a toy for her. When she told me that I was sad, Jackie would always wait for toys. Jackie said she rarely got a chance to go outside to play because she had to take care of us first. Mom always told her she was the oldest and had to help her. Mom promised Jackie her turn was coming. Jackie was sad. I was too. I told her she could have my toy and not to cry.

Someone came to the door and knocked. Jackie and Craig had been playing all night like it was dad. It seemed that whatever we went through we always found reasons to laugh and be happy. We knew dad was driving from Chicago to get us but, we didn't know what time to expect him. We waited anxiously for him to show up. Jackie made me and Oliviodale take a bath while we waited. We heard another hard knock at the door, this time it sounded different. Then we heard a man's voice - it was daddy! We jumped out the tub butt naked and ran into the front room. Oliviodale and I jumped into dad's arms full of excitement and joy. Jackie and Craig were running around the kitchen excited; they knew we were about to leave. Daddy was glad to find us safe. He packed the few things we had, placed them in the car, and we left.

We cried that night. I wanted my mom. We talked about the toys in the closet we didn't get a chance to open for Christmas. Dad was taking us back to Mississippi to our great-grandmother's house again. We were sad. We were happy to see dad, but sad to leave without knowing when we would see our mom again.

DIRTY OLD MEN

Our father was a great provider, and he did as much as he could with the help of our great-grandmother. It was hard to find a good woman that was willing to take care of four children. After daddy divorced, he didn't trust another woman around us.

Great-grandmother didn't have a telephone, the only way dad could see how we were doing was to call the white man at the corner store, Mr. Marlow, or write us a letter, but he didn't often write unless he was mailing money.

Our father wasn't bad. He was described by many to be a good man and hard worker and provider. Why didn't great-grandmother ever say we were going to be just like him? I'm grateful that I didn't let her negative wishes penetrate in my head.

Jackie got a job working for Mr. Marlow at the store in town. One-day Mr. Marlow told my sister she owed him money and that she could pay him back by having sex with him.

Mom had written my sister a letter telling her she would be coming home soon, and if she could get some money, she was going to come and get us. My sister went to work for Mr. Marlow the next day and took all his money out of the safe. Jackie said, she did it because she wanted mom to come get us. When mom arrived, we were all excited. Jackie gave her an envelope with the money in it. Daddy didn't know what was going on. The same man that was telling daddy we were doing all right was the same man that was molesting my sister.

Great-grandmother let me ride to church with Mr. Smith, the cookie man, and he would tell me that he would give me cookies if I let him touch me. He was tall, dark-skinned, thick and a partially bald head; he was one of the deacons in the Church. The church was called Squirrel Lake Church of God in Christ. It was a little wooden church located in the woods and seated 25 people. They put him out of the church because he had gotten a 16 years old girl pregnant. She lost the baby. It was horrible that something so bad had to happen before the people in the church believed that we were telling the truth about the dirty old man.

Justice was met. He was later locked up for taking advantage of a minor. Great-grandmother Ella took us to church Sunday, Monday, Tuesday, Wednesday, Thursday, Friday, and Saturday.

I will never forget the day she was outside hanging clothes on the clothes line and my little puppy went up to her to play. As I watched out of the window, he wiggled his tail in a friendly manner. I loved that little puppy; he was only 6 weeks old. She took her garden tool and hit him twice. He fell over to the side. I ran outside to pick him up, but he was dead. She told me to go back in the house and justified why she killed my puppy. That's why when she went to town Oliviodale, and I shot at her cat with his b.b. gun. I disliked her for killing my puppy, and I was very angry with her for a long time. It seemed that the few things we loved were always taken from us.

ALTAR CALL

One Sunday we went to church and were told to come to the altar to pray. Everybody went to the altar to pray. I was praying, but I didn't know what to pray for. I wanted my momma and my daddy, but I didn't feel praying was going to get them for me. I prayed for God to send my parent's home once before, but they hadn't come, so I didn't know what to pray for. Oliviodale, my youngest brother, was on his knees while all the other church members had gotten up from the altar except Oliviodale. He stayed on his knees for at least 15 additional minutes. My great-grandmother got up and started praising him, and shouting saying I know I raised my great-grandchildren to serve God. She was bragging. The pastor came down from the pulpit and bragged about how good of a job she had done raising us. My brother remained on his knees praying. One of the deacons came down and touched him on his shoulder. Oliviodale fell back and was snoring. Oliviodale wasn't praying he was sleeping. The whole church laughed at my brother. My great-grandmother was embarrassed and shame. Oliviodale got a beating that night, because he had embarrassed great-grandmother.

One other occasion we went to church and great-grandmother said we had to get on the mourning bench to seek the Holy Ghost. The mourning bench was a bench you sat on until the Holy Ghost came and healed you from all your sins. All of us got on the mourning bench - we mourned and mourned and mourned, but it wasn't for the Holy Ghost, it was for our mom or dad to come for us. My sister started to shout, because she had gotten the Holy Ghost, my brother Craig fell on the floor screaming and shouting, because he had gotten the Holy Ghost and Oliviodale was running around the benches because, he had gotten the Holy Ghost too. I waited and waited and waited for the Holy Ghost, but it wouldn't come. My great-grandmother had already told us that we better not fake it and she said we better keep our eyes closed while waiting. My eyes were closed, but I was peeping. If I got the Holy Ghost, I wanted to see what it looked like. She used her finger and beckoned for me to come over to the bench where she was sitting. Not thinking, I went jumping and shouting over to her, but I forgot I wasn't supposed to have my eyes opened. My great-grandmother was embarrassed, and she took me outside and whipped me with a long switch. We laugh as we talked about that day at church. Jackie said she just wanted her to shut up. Craig said he didn't want to hear her fuss when we return home. Olivodale said, he was having fun and didn't want to fall to sleep again. I wanted it to be over with, because I was tired of all the screaming and shouting.

Oliviodale would urinate in the bed; he said he tried to hold it but couldn't. The little old lady, next door to us, told great-grandmother to feed him some liver to make his bladder stronger, but instead, great-grandmother would whip him. It seemed that everybody picked on Oliviodale. My great-grandmother, my stepmother, and even mom accused him of doing things he hadn't done. Oliviodale hated our great-grandmother. He said, I hated her twice. I hated her for beating morals and God into us so brutally. My sister Jackie said, she hated her because she talked about our mother. Jackie said she thought God hated her. I told her, "Jackie God doesn't hate you, because you're my big sister," Craig said, "It seems like great-grandmother whipped me for nothing." I was the youngest child, and I spoke my mind. I always said what I felt. I told her to please just go away and leave me alone.

DON'T FORGET US MOM

My oldest brother said he remembers writing mom, and she would write him back occasionally and tell him she loved us. My brother said he didn't want her to forget about us. My mom got out of jail and came to Darling to get us again. Not knowing where we were going to live, we were happy to be with our mom, and we were glad to see her. We remembered daddy saying how beautiful mom was when they got married and how he wished she would get herself together. We were looking for that mother that dad told us about. She brought us back to Memphis, and we stayed in different hotels. We lived in a hotel on Elvis Presley Street with our mom and a man named Fred. They both had gotten out of jail for stealing and forging checks. They met up in Memphis.

We were all in the room excited. Oliviodale and I were playing with his truck on the floor, and mom thought he was peeping through the key hole.

She whipped him for peeping. I didn't get a whipping, but I was the one peeping in the key-hole, and I was the one that saw mom and one of her friends, wrap Fred's arm with a rubber band and stick the needle of heroin in his arm. To this day I'm afraid of needles. Fred died that night. Mom and Bertha were in the room trying to revive him. They took all his clothes off and took him outside and walked him up and down the streets, until he became conscious. Mom and her friend, walked him naked for hours until he started coughing and throwing up mucous. We left the hotel that night and moved not far to another hotel. I remembered telling mom we were leaving our new clothes. She said, "don't worry about those clothes, I'll get you some more – we got to go". We were on the run again. We left our clothes. Mom told us we would get more, and we did. I thought we were rich, because mom always got new, name brand clothes when they went out shoplifting. I was older now and realized we weren't rich. I remembered telling mom stealing was wrong. She told me God understood. I told her no he didn't. I told her what great-grandmother told us and that was mom you need God in your life. She looked at me with tears in her eyes.

THE ROOMING HOUSE

I recalled living in the rooming house on Butler Street. It was another raggedy neighborhood. There were lots of people coming in and out of this house. Some of them were disgusting, but some were just down on their luck. However; most of them would occasionally watch out for us while mom was gone. People sold bootlegged whiskey, cigarettes, and all kinds of stuff in the house. A partially blind man, sit in the hallway and smoked cigarettes. We had to walk past him to go to our room. Every time I went passed him; he would try to grab me. He was a dirty old man, and I didn't want him touching me, so I ran fast pass him to keep him from touching me. He was married to a woman that I later called my Godmother. She watched us periodically when mom was gone with friends. She didn't know her partially blind husband was trying to touch me under my dress. One day as I ran to pass him, and I slipped and felled on the floor furnace. I burned my back very bad. Mom wasn't there, the old people in the rooming house bandaged my back and told me I would be okay. When asked, how I burned my back, Mr. Avery said I was running down the hall and fell because I was being bad. He didn't tell them I was running to keep him from putting his dirty hands on me. I told him if he tried to touch me again I was going to tell his wife. After that, he left me alone, but I still told his wife. She promised me he would never again threaten to do anything to me.

He took my brothers downtown to beg for change. They stood on the streets with him and asked for money. One day we all went downtown without Mr. Avery and begged for money. Craig said he was going to keep some of the money to buy mom some raisins for her birthday. She loved raisins. When Craig gave her the raisins for her birthday gift she was surprised. The gift made her happy.

There were times that mom left us in the rooming house unattended. We would go downtown and look at the lights or go to the Hippodrome skating rink at night by ourselves. We managed to get in free, because we learned how to smile like our mother. Our smile helped us to get into a lot of places free. We moved from the rooming house and ended up in different people houses mom knew.

Mom went out to party and left us with some lady up the street. Mrs. Rosie, my godmother, separated from Mr. Avery, because she learned he had been molesting young girls. She beat him with a belt. It was funny because he was trying to run, but he couldn't, because he was in a wheelchair and blind. Mrs. Rosie moved in some apartments on Bellevue Street near the rooming house. I went to stay with her for a while. Oliviodale went to stay with his Godmother, Bessie for a while. Jackie went to stay with her Godmother, and Craig stayed with mom. We all had Godmothers that helped mom out from time to time.

THE VILLAGE

      I realized now that I'm older the meaning and importance of the Village. It truly takes the community to be concerned about the least fortunate children. We were four little children with two beautiful parents that had no idea that they would run into the tragic lifestyle they did. We were thankful for our auntie and the people in the hood that watched over us. I guess that's why I was so serious about sharing the truth of my life, because I promised that little girl that I was coming back. It's still in my head that I promised her I would be back. I did go back to the apartments, but when I got there, they weren't there anymore. The building had been torn down, and there was only a vacant lot. Those memories had been torn down, but they will forever be memories in my heart. Those children gave me reasons to write a story of truth hoping that our story would help other children and families that may have experienced some of the same things we had. It was my hope that maybe the children would one day pick up my book and read it.

I'M TOO YOUNG
TO BE TIRED

Mom rented another apartment and came to get us from our Godmothers. We stayed in the apartments for two weeks. She dropped us off at school one day, and told my sister Jackie to take care of us, because she had to go to jail. My sister was 12, my brother Craig was 11, Oliviodale was 10, and I was 8. My sister didn't know where we were going to stay that night or what we were going to eat. She was scared and sad. At the end of the school day, she went to the office and told the principal that our mom was gone to jail. We didn't have a clue what was going to happen to us. As we prepared to leave the school, we were called to the office where several police officers were waiting for us. They asked a few questions that we were not able to answer. One question was, where was our mother? The other questions asked was, where is your dad? The last one was, were we staying at home alone? I told them we were staying home alone because our mother was gone, and our daddy was in Chicago. They put us in the back seat of the car and off we went. The other children watched the police load us up, they laughed and said we were "wanted". The police took us away. We all cried. It was a very embarrassing experience.

THE ORPHANAGE HOME

I often wondered why my dad didn't take us from the bad environments we were staying in. My sister blamed herself for a long time. She said it was her fault that we had been taken to Juvenile Court. We stayed in Juvenile Court for over 2 weeks, and they transported us to the orphanage home.

The people were friendly at the orphanage home. There were other children to play with, and we had our own rooms. I felt like we were at a resort. I felt like we were at Walt Disney Land. It was clean; we had clean clothes, food to eat and toys to play with - we had structure. Our main concern was that we weren't separated. We made it clear amongst one another that we would not let anyone separate us, and if someone wanted to adopt one of us, they had to adopt all of us. Most people weren't looking for older children to adopt. I remembered a couple requiring of me. I made sure they knew I had a sister and two brothers. I told one lady that if she took me from my sister and brothers, I would be a very bad little girl. She never came back to inquire about adopting me. Our concern was never to be separated.

We stayed in the orphanage home for three weeks. This time mom had gone to jail for robbery. South Virginia is where my mom served four years for attempting to rob a bank. Mom was so high off drugs that day; she went into the bank with a note that read "You're being robbed". "Give me all your money". Fred was outside in the getaway car, but they didn't get away. Policemen came from everywhere and again she was taken to jail.

BACK TO GREAT GRAND MOM HOUSE

At age of 9 in 1970, we were back with our father in Chicago. Daddy came to the orphanage to get us. Daddy never expressed his pain - he dealt with it inwardly and did a good job of it. He came to get us, and we went back to Chicago with him for a few weeks. Daddy didn't have help, so he called great-grandmother to let her know he was bringing us back to Mississippi. I was tired of going from place to place. All I wanted was a normal life. If we weren't on the run with our mother, we were going back and forward with our dad to Chicago and then to Mississippi to our great-grandmother. I decided I would pray. I prayed that God would soon settle us down so that we could live a normal life. I prayed that my mother would get herself together and be free of drugs and alcohol. I prayed that dad would soon find help, so he wouldn't have to take us back to great-grandmother house. Mom got out of jail again and came for us.

THE CONSEQUENCES
OF POOR CHOICES

We moved in with Jay-Jay, one of mom's friends that lived in the Foot Homes projects. Jay-Jay was like an aunt to us and a sister to mom. Mom and Jay-Jay met in the streets while being ladies of the night. Jay-Jay didn't have a mother or father, and she and mom hit it off and bonded like sisters. They helped one another and could talk about their pains with one another.

Jay-Jay was a good person that did bad things. She sold bags of weed for $5 and $10. Sometimes we sold it for her. If someone dropped by and needed a bag, we knew where the weed was and how much it cost. We did as she would have done and that was sold the weed and charged them. We didn't give the money to Jay Jay. We would spend it going to the skating rink, or we would get some junk food. They would always say do as they tell us to do and not as we see them do, but that wasn't working. We were beginning to do what we saw them do.

Jay-Jay had a little girl, she was bi-racial, and one of the attorneys she dated was her father. She said she had unprotected sex one night because she didn't have a condom. She said she needed the money and, so she took the chance, but didn't consider the consequences and got pregnant. When she reached out to him to let him know that she had gotten pregnant with a child, he rejected the child. She was our baby, and we watched over her. We took her with us everywhere we went. It was something about our family; we learned to stick together regardless of what the circumstances were.

One day a drug deal went bad. Mom, Oliviodale and I and a few of mom's men friends were sitting in the front room when a man came to the apartment and started shooting. He got in, and we ran; he went upstairs looking for one of mom's friend's, but couldn't find her, so he shot up the bedroom. We were trained to hide dope in a hole outside and cover it up with dirt. So, when the man came in, we took the bags of weed, ran and hid it in the dirt. Everybody scattered throughout the house.

I remembered my sister Jackie dressing me and sending me off to school. She dressed me in a plaid dress with navy blue strapped shoes and white laced socks. I felt like I was going to a prestigious school, although I was going to a school in my "hood" called Vance Elementary. I felt loved. I felt pretty. I prayed daily for my mother to be sane. Day and night, I prayed that one day my mother struggles would be over. My sister was a little girl too, but she was the oldest and felt obligated to take care of us. I was sad to hear all the stories of how she never got the chance to be a little girl. I grew up knowing that if I were ever successful, I would share my success with her. After all, she had made many attempts to protect me as the youngest child in the family.

One of mom's friends, died of lupus. She was Jay, Jay's sister. We knew that Jay-Jay would be leaving soon for California. Jay-Jay wasn't our biological aunt, but she was a part of what we called our extended family. She shared the little she had with us. Mom took over the apartment when Jay-Jay left and moved an old man in named Mr. Chuck. He received a disability check; mom let him stay, because he helped to pay the rent. Mom didn't have a job; she used her street sense to make a living. She would go out to the cafés and get drunk. Her lifestyle had begun to ruin her peachy colored skin, wavy hair, brown hazel eyes and her beautiful smile. She began to look bad from all the drugs, alcohol and beatings.

DEADLY FIGHTS

Mom often went to the café on Polk and Walnut off Crump Street. One-day mom and this man were coming out of the café arguing and stabbing at each other with butcher knives. He beat mom on the outside of the café. She was on the sidewalk bleeding, but she wouldn't go to the hospital. She came to the apartment, cleaned herself up, got herself a drink and said she would be alright. She was anxious to go back and get him. She kept saying "I'm going to get him." It was painful seeing mom get beat on, but there was nothing we could do, because most of the time mom would have tricked someone out of their money or provoked the fight.

Chuck and mom got into an argument one night about his check. Mom told him he had to get out. He said he wasn't going, because he had paid his money to stay. Mom called the police. The police came in, and Chuck had a gun. The police told him to put his hands up, but Chuck reached down and grabbed the gun instead. The gun went off and shot the police officer, and the police shot Chuck. Oliviodale and Craig saw the shooting take place, I heard it. My sister, Jackie wasn't there. Craig said he was afraid he was going to get shot. Oliviodale said he sat up in the bed in shock, I ran through the room screaming, because blood was on the floor and the bed. I was frightened. We all ran outside and slid down the pole - my heart was rushing fast.

NASTY

Mom never lost contact with the different men she dated. She occasionally called on Zack and Mr. Smitty for money to help pay her bills. Mr. Smitty would see me outside playing and offer me money to let him do nasty things to me. I told him no several times, but one time he offered me $15, we were hungry, mom was gone out in the streets on one of her binges. I met him at his house down the streets. I closed my eyes as he licked me; I said to myself I wish he would hurry up. When he finished, he said I'll see you next week? I went back to the house, but Craig and Jackie were gone. I bought Oliviodale and myself a hamburger and some candy and kept the change. I felt horrible. I was only 10 years old and was already picking up bad habits from those women in my life.

Mom told my sister that her friend, Zack had a job for her at the sundry and she needed to work, so she went to work for Zack. One day the sundry was robbed. Zack said his friends said it was Fred, mom's old boyfriend. Jackie admitted that the robber looked like Fred, but he had on a black mask, and she wasn't sure if it was Fred or not. Mom was out to get revenge. Zack said my sister had to give up her check and sex because it was her fault. He molested her at the very young age of 14. He said she knew who robbed the store and she was responsible.

Jackie was going through Foote Homes on several occasions to get to school where there would be four boys that would throw bottles at her. As she ran, they chased after her. One day they took her into a vacant apartment and raped her. She said she was frightened for her life. Shortly after she was raped, she learned she was pregnant and didn't know whose baby it was. Mom said the baby was her male friend, Zack. My sister said she tried to get an abortion, because truly she didn't know if it was the dirty old man Zack or the dirty boys that raped her. Momma didn't know what was going on most of the time. She was busy doing her thing drinking and drugging. One-night Jackie was out in the streets and began to hurt. She got into a vacant car and laid there. A man found her and took her to the hospital where the baby was born dead. These things should have never happened to either of us. We were children. The cycle of abuse was continuing.

Tears streamed down my eyes as I continued to write. I wanted to go back and find all of them; I wanted revenge. However, Zack was dead. Fred was dead, Shorty was dead, Mr. Marlow was dead, Smitty was dead, and several of those boys were dead. I told my sister I was sorry that those bad things had happened to her. She looked at me and said, "I did all I could to keep you from those bad things," and she said I didn't want to tell you what was happening to me, because you were too young to understand." I said to her "I'm a big girl now and I can handle it."

She didn't know that I too had been affected by the dirty old men that came around. Mr. Avery, the blind man, was dead, and the deacon that came to pick us up for the church was dead. As I told my sister about the dirty old men that had taken advantage of me, she began to cry. I told her it wasn't her fault. Really it wasn't anybody to blame. Mom was having a very bad time in her life, and we were subject to having a bad time also. Yes, it hurt, but I loved my mother so much I never blamed her. It was obvious mom was sick. We prayed and prayed that she would heal. We needed her to heal so that we could heal.

DAD CAME FOR US

Jay-Jay called dad from California and told him to come for us, because she believed we were being abused. She told him, mom was still using drugs and abusing alcohol. He and another lady drove to Memphis to get us. My sister was gone that night. She was out looking for mom. Dad waited and waited for her to come home – he said he would have to leave soon, because he had to return to work that next morning. As we were preparing our things to leave Jackie finally came in the house. She was excited to see dad, but not sure about his friend. When dad told her, he was there to take us with him; she began to cry. She didn't want to leave until she found mom.

Mom had been gone all day, and Jackie was worried. While dad was in the back with us, she left the house, and didn't return. Dad and his new lady friend loaded Craig, Olivodale and my things in the car and off to Chicago we went again. My sister was left in Memphis all alone searching for mom. I worried about her because, she was only 16. I was 12 at the time.

Dad introduced us to his new girlfriend. She was young, only 25 years old. We weren't excited about meeting her, because we thought she was another one of those women that wanted daddy all for herself. She did all she could to make us comfortable. As we drove to Chicago, she tried to talk to us. She asked questions and made jokes, but we said nothing. It was hard to trust step parents, because we had experienced so many bad things with both the men and women that came in our lives.

We were excited to arrive to dad's house. It was a big three-story home. We had never seen a house that big. I had my own bedroom, the boys had their own bedrooms, and even though Jackie wasn't there, she had her own bedroom too. The refrigerator was full of food, and it was nice and clean. Dad's new girlfriend showed us where everything was and off to sleep we went. I was so happy to be in a place where I felt safe finally.

I would wash the dishes, make the beds, mop the floors and vacuum the rooms. The boys would take out the garbage and keep dad and his new girlfriend car clean. They didn't have to ask us to do it; we did it because we appreciated being in a home where we felt safe. Dad gave us all an allowance if we did our chores without being asked.

Regardless of the shotgun houses, apartments and hotels we stayed in with mom, she taught us to keep them clean, and we did. Even though great-grandmother was mean and strict, I never forgot how she taught us to pray.

PRAYER WORKS

I missed my sister a lot while in Chicago. One night while sitting in my bedroom, I thought about all the time's great-grandmother told us that prayer worked and I said a prayer that my sister would call and let us know if she was okay. Shortly after I prayed, the telephone rang. Daddy was sleep, and Margaret was too. I sneaked into the front room and answered the telephone. It was Jackie! I was excited to hear her voice. Tears began to run down my eyes. I caught my breath and said hello. She immediately asked were we okay? I answered, "Yes". I asked her where was she and why didn't she come back to the house that night dad came for us? She said, she was okay, but didn't return, because she wanted to find mom. She said she didn't find her until 6 months later. She said, she had been staying in a mechanic shop, sleeping on their dirty couch. She said, she waited until they closed shop and snuck through the open window. She told me she was frightened, because the mechanic shop had lots of old truck parts and cars in the backyard. I asked her did the owners know she was sleeping there. She said, no they didn't. She said, one day she overslept, and one of the guys came in and caught her sleeping. I was scared to hear what else happened. I asked, "What did he do?" She said, nothing. She said she told him she had been looking for mom and didn't have anywhere to go. She told the guy that daddy had come for us, but left her in Memphis. The guy let her stay until she found mom.

She said, when she found mom she was living with this big and bald man. He did yard work for a living. Jackie said, mom had accused her before, and she wasn't going to be accused again, so she didn't stay with mom. She told me she met some guy and moved in with him. I asked her to come to Chicago. She said she would think about it. Then she said she had to go. I threw kisses through the telephone and said good-bye. That night I got on my knees and told God thanks for taking care of my sister and thanks for letting her call. That night was the beginning to me believing in the power of prayer.

DAD FOUND A HELPMATE

Margaret was off to herself and didn't have much to say. She cooked for us and took us shopping for clothes. She made sure we got to school on time, and we ate three meals a day. Regardless of how nice she was to us, we didn't trust her. We thought her being nice to us was too good to be true because, we had been mistreated by one stepmother, and we had been taken advantage of by the dirty old men that came around momma, and great-grandmother. I didn't want her to be my friend or my mother. I never wanted our mom's men to be my daddy, and I never wanted our daddy's women to be my mom. We made it hard for dad's new friend, because we didn't allow her to be our friend or our mom. She thought we were being mean little children, but she didn't know the extent to which we had experience abuse and neglect. I could tell by us being mean to dad's friend it put a lot of stress on him. He didn't know what to do. He cared for her, and he cared for us. He wanted us to get alone.

Margaret had one son who was being raised by her mother. He would come over on the weekends occasionally to visit. We never got to know him, because when he came to visit, he didn't stay long. One night he was out with some friends, and someone murdered him. They shot him 3 times in the face. It was a sad night for Margaret when the police called the house. I will never forget the call. They telephone ranged, I answered, and the police identified himself and asked to speak with Margaret. It sounded like trouble, but Olivodale was in the house. I gave her the telephone. She took it. She was quiet at first, and then suddenly, she began to scream and run around the house. She was crying and saying she couldn't believe they had killed her son. My brother Olivodale and dad went with her to identify the body. I realized that night that she didn't have to help dad raise us, she could have been raising her own son, but she loved dad so much she stayed with him and helped with us. She later told us she felt guilty when her son got murdered, because she was helping dad raise his four children while her mother was taking care of her only son. She later learned that my father had two more daughters by another woman. Margaret's world took a drastic turn. She was only twenty-five years old and had lost her only child but, yet she found enough love in her heart to help dad with the six of his children. She went into a depression and isolated herself from everyone.

She had a daily routine. She went to work, came home, cooked our food and went to her room, crawled into the bed and shut her door. One day I sat on the outside of her door and listened to her cry. It was sad to hear her moan. Now that I'm an adult it hurts, even more, to think of how mean we were to the woman that helped my dad and mother raise us.

Dad at the time was working and providing for us and felt that was enough. We never talked to him about the abuse we had experienced while we were with mom or great-grandmother. He was too busy working and providing our needs to listen to our problems. I didn't have any complaints; I was happy to be with him. None of us showed Margaret any sympathy when her son died; we swept it under the rug as we did with most painful things. Growing up as children we learn to deal with pain; it was almost normal for us. I finally went in one night when I heard her crying and hugged her. I told her how much I loved her and how grateful I was for all the things she had done for us. I said a prayer for her that night, because after all had it not been for Margaret, we would be stuck at great-grandmother house.

Margaret smiled and said thanks.

DEATH BROUGHT
US CLOSER

Margaret and Oliviodale became closer after her son's death. She called on him for everything, and he was always available. I could only assume maybe it was because she had lost her son. Perhaps it was because she too heard the rumor that Oliviodale wasn't my dad's biological son. I soon became very close to her. I wonder if she knew a secret about me, because we also became very close.

Margaret needed something we didn't know how to give, and that was love. We had seen our mother experience so much pain that we thought it was the way of life. Margaret never beat us, and that was all we wanted from her. I didn't miss mom as bad – I adjusted and accepted her as dad's wife. I began to show her love.

FAST MONEY

Oliviodale could do no wrong in Margaret's eyes. He was making money singing in shows as the "Blues Brothers," and he also worked a paper route. One night he robbed the hardware store up the streets. He hid all the stolen tools in his car. The police came and knocked at the door looking for him; he was in the basement hiding. Margaret told the police that he had been in the house all night; however, the next day the police returned, and he went to jail. Dad went to get him out of jail. Dad was convinced that his son, Oliviodale didn't rob the store, but Margaret said she knew that Olivodale robbed the store, but she never told dad. She said she always worried hoping Olivodale didn't get into trouble. I asked him why he did that; he said he wanted some quick cash. I asked him how was jail? He said he never wanted to revisit jail. After all, mom had shown us what getting quick cash had done for her? He agreed.

Craig was working for Xerox in the computer department. He was a lot like dad, quiet and stayed off to himself. He never expressed his pain. He never let any of us know what was going on with him, he kept it inside, and he stayed out of trouble.

Margaret appreciated me cleaning the house.

She surprised me several times by taking me shopping. Often, when I would clean, I wouldn't let anyone sit on the couches or walk on the cleanly mopped floors. Margaret would laugh, dad just shook his head. I was happy to be in a beautiful home, and I wanted it to stay clean. After all, I never forgot what mom told us about keeping our home clean.

SHE TRUSTED NO ONE

Jackie came to visit us in Chicago, but she didn't stay long. Margaret said, Jackie took her credit cards and charged airline tickets to travel to California where that boy was that she fell in love with. Jackie wasn't sure about anything or anyone. Jackie said everyone had done mean things to her. She said great-grandma told her when she was a little girl that God hated her, mom had accused her of having sexual encounters with her men, and dad girlfriend taught her how to smoke cigarettes. She said she wasn't sure if anyone loved her. I recall Jackie going to a palm reader to see what her future was going to be like. I was frightened as I waited in the car. There were wind chimes and bottles all over the yard. When Jackie returned to the car, I asked,

"Jackie, who did you go in there to visit?" She said, I visit a lady that read my palm. I was young and didn't have any idea what a palm reader was.

Margaret thought Jackie was practicing witchcraft to separate her and dad, but she wasn't practicing witchcraft. She said, she went to the fortune teller praying that she would tell her she was going to have a better future. She said, she was hoping the fortune teller would tell her someone loved her. Jackie said, she was angry that she had been left in Memphis with nowhere to go. I told her "Daddy didn't leave you, he waited and waited for you to return, but you didn't come back." She felt a little better after I shared the truth with her, but she was still angry and hurt. As Jackie and I sat talking about those days, I told her perhaps she should have told dad how she felt about that night. Perhaps if she had told him, she wouldn't feel like she felt. She said, "I just left it alone".

STAY TOGETHER

One of many lessons we learned through it all was to stick together regardless of whatever we were going through. I learned to love my siblings, and I would fight for them. I was the youngest out of the four of us, and they did all they could to protect me. I grew up with a desire to make my siblings lives better; I felt like I owed them something. That something was to be successful and help them with their pain.

I remembered one day while in Chicago in middle school some Mexican boys were going to jump Oliviodale. They had guns and were going to throw him out the window. I came around the corner and saw them holding my brother towards the window. I asked one of the guys what are you doing to my brother? He said none of my business and continued to hit him. I took off my shoes, drop my books and began to swing. I found whatever I could and beat the devil out of them. I told them if they were going to throw my brother out of the window, they had to throw me out the window too. Another cycle repeated itself. My mother and her brother were very close, and my brother I were close also. I wasn't very close to my sister, but I would fight for her.

There was another time that Oliviodale got to fighting with a big tall, tuff boy in the neighborhood named Nonny-Boy. He was a bully, and everybody was afraid of him. He had taken Oliviodale's ice cream cone. I came outside, and they were fighting. I jumped in the fight. Whenever there was a fight that involved my siblings, I jumped in it. I told Jackie about the story she said, one thing Mom told her to do was stick together. Somehow, we manage to do just that. Stick together.

IN MY FATHER'S HOUSE

In my father's house, our chores were to clean the house, go to school, be in the house before dark, and obey his rules. We had structure. I didn't have to worry about the loud outburst anymore, because dad didn't fight women, he wasn't raised to put his hands-on women. I was happy that we didn't worry any longer about our things being put out on the streets. Dad took on two jobs to provide us with a quality lifestyle.

One day I went fishing with one of the old men who owned a barber shop down the streets from my father's house. He said he was going to give me money and take me shopping. Dad found out I had shot hooky from school and went fishing with the old man. Dad was so mad; he threatened to beat me and the man with a baseball bat. My dad had never whipped me before, and I was scared to death. That was the last time I was seen hanging around any dirty old men.

We lived in the suburbs of Chicago in a nice two-story house with a fenced in back yard. We rode in dad's new cars, and all they asked of us was to go to school, be respectful and do our chores. Dad and our stepmother did the rest. They were both great providers; they showed us how to live an honest life. It was a great feeling to be stable. We no longer witnessed the devastation of domestic violence, drugs, alcohol abuse, molestation, and theft.

In 1976 dad received a telephone call that my great-grandmother Ella had died. I was 15 about to turn 16. I was glad she had died, because I knew that my dad could never take us back to her again. Oliviodale said, he was glad she had died too, Craig said he felt no remorse and Jackie said she was happy she wouldn't have to hear that mess about "you're going to be just like your mom". We were all happy that we wouldn't have to return to her. I remembered going to the funeral home to visit her body, but didn't one tear drop from my eyes. I was running up and down the streets repeating out loud, "The wicked witch has died." It seemed that the wind knew she was dead because it was very windy outside that day. I felt like Dorothy on the Wizard of Oz. I was running down the streets shouting, "No more pain from that old lady. No more pain! The wicked witch is dead. "

Mom had been out of prison for a year. She was living in Memphis on Southern in a duplex with the same man named Marcus. My sister had given birth to her first baby girl; she was traveling back and forward from Memphis to California. I missed her being around. When I turned 16, I asked my dad if I could go and live with my mother in Memphis for a little while. He said, yes after just a little thought. Dad never said bad things about mom, and mom never said bad things about dad. I was concerned, because I had grown accustomed to living in a middle-class environment. Our lifestyle was totally different from that of living in the hood, surrounded by poverty. I wasn't sure what I was about to get myself into, but I was willing to take the risk just to be with the woman that I called mom.

TEENAGE PREGNANCY

At the early age of 16, I was off to Memphis, Tennessee to start a new life with my mother, and it was exciting. The summer came, and I packed my bags to stay with mom. I was looking forward to bonding with her, and helping her to get herself together. I remembered getting on the Greyhound bus; it was a bitter sweet moment. I was confused. It was sweet that I was off to see mom, but bitter that I was leaving my dad. Dad put my bags at the bottom of the bus, he gave me some cash, a big hug, and told me to be a good girl. I promised him I would as I was getting on the bus. It seemed like it was taking the bus forever to get to Memphis. I dozed off to sleep, and when I awaken, we were in Memphis. I got off the bus anticipating what to expect. I hadn't seen her in years. She drove up in a raggedy red pickup truck, load with dirt on the back bed. I recognize her immediately because she had that beautiful smile on her face. I rushed, gathered my bags and ran to hugged her. I was excited to see her, and she was excited to see me. She hugged me for a long time. Neither one of us wanted to let go of one another. I smelled alcohol on her breath, but she didn't appear drunk. We pulled up to a little red and white house and walked in. I was happy to see that things were organized and clean. I put my bags down and made myself at home.

I was surprised when mom's friend came around the corner and introduced himself to me. I said hi, he spoke and went to his room. I was old enough to beat the living cow out of him if he stepped out of line. Mom and I sat on the sofa and talked for hours until we both felled asleep. I asked her how things were; she told me everything was okay. She told me she was still drinking and admitted she needed help. She apologized for leaving us. I told her how much I missed her and how glad I was that we were back together again. I was happy that we could pick up from where we left off. It didn't take long for mom and me to bond. We talked about some devastating things she had experienced. Mom began to cry, and I cried with her because some of the things that happened to her had affected me. She shared with me some of the habits she was battling with and apologize for those things that had happened to me.

She was angry, because she didn't have a clue that some of the stuff I shared with her had happened to us.

Mom made me feel I could trust her with my deepest secrets, because she never blamed me for the things that happened. Nor did I blame her. I had concluded that mom was sickly intoxicated. I told mom I was ready to start over again and I wanted to make the best of our time together.

In Chicago, I didn't have anyone to talk to about sex, my sister wasn't around often, and I wasn't comfortable with telling Margaret or Dad that I had a boyfriend. We had dated for several months. He was sad when I told him I would be leaving for Memphis. I went over to his house before leaving to say my goodbyes. We got intimate that night before I left for the bus station. I was smart that I had started on birth control, because the last thing I wanted to do was get pregnant.

I HAD A PLAN

I had a plan. My plan was to come to Memphis, finish high school and attend college so that I could help my mother get herself together. I wanted to make my parents proud of me, but most of all, I wanted to stop the generational curses and dysfunctional cycles from repeating in my life. I wanted my lifestyle to be different, and I didn't want to live in poverty. I didn't want to fall into the same traps mom had experienced. There were several things I vowed; I would never tolerate or do. I said, I would never be in an abusive relationship. Nor did I want to ever be involved in an alcoholic or drug driven relationship. The other vow I made was not to get pregnant before I finished college, married and started a career for myself. I witnessed the stress that mom and dad had under-gone from getting pregnant at the young teenage of 16 and 18. They both said they loved all of us. However, mom said the consequences of her having children at such a tender age caused her lots of pain. She said, things got really bad when she and dad separated. She told me regardless of what happened they remained best friends. She said, once they separated she started looking for love in all the wrong places. I asked her if she could give us back, would she? She said, of course not. I watched my mother struggle with so many things. It was my promise to do the opposite of those things that hurt her. I wanted revenge and the only way I could get it was to become a curse breaker. I had work to do. I had to avoid all the traps mom had fallen into that contributed to her having a dysfunctional lifestyle.

I was happy to enroll in school and excited to be on my way to finishing my senior year in Tennessee with my mother. Mom and I had talked about my plans for College. I was off to a good start. The next morning, I went to school registered for my senior classes, there stood this handsome guy in the office, he kept staring at me, and I kept staring at him. I wanted to speak to him, but I was shy, he passed me and didn't say anything, so I kept going.

The next day I returned to school, to inquire about getting on the cheerleader team, he walked in to get his jersey. Oh my god! I was about to faint, but I kept my composure. One of the school band leaders walked in and began to talk with him about the drums he would be playing. I was impressed that he played in the band and also, he was on the A basketball team. The secretary gave me the information I needed to try out for the cheerleader squad, and I proceeded to leave out the door. As I was leaving, he rushed to grab the door. I was bashful, but I didn't hesitate to say thanks for being a gentleman. As I was walking towards my car, he asked if I had a boyfriend. I smiled and said I use too. He asked did I have a moment. I told him yes. So, I went over and talked more about the relationship I use to have. I then asked him if he had a girlfriend. He said not anymore. I told him I didn't believe him, because he was so good looking that it was hard to see how he would be single. He went on to explain that they had broken up, because she was moving out of town. I was shocked! I told him that was the same reason my boyfriend and I was no longer dating. He was shocked that I was from Chicago. He asked me if he could take me out on a date. I said, "Yes." I blushed. I returned home excited to tell mom. She was okay with me having a boyfriend, but she reminded me of what dad and Margaret told me and that was be a good girl and don't bring my fast tail to Memphis and get pregnant.

TEENAGE SEX

We dated a little while; he was the perfect gentleman. He never called my house after 10:00 pm unless we had agreed. We went out on dates to dinners, movies, games, museums and the carnivals. I enjoyed him, because we did simple things together and still had fun. One of the simple things we did was road on the school bus to and from the games together. I was excited that he wanted me to meet his parents, because I had been told if a guy takes a girl home to meet his parents, he liked her. We set a date, and he took me over for dinner. His mother and father were nice. We were off to a good start.

I liked him, and he liked me. One night he came over, we were alone. He sat next to me, and we talked about our feelings for one another. He touched me, and I touched him. Next, he kissed me, and I kissed him back. The kiss led to touching and the touching led to sex. The next month, I missed my cycle. I prayed that I was just late coming on and waited and waited and waited but my cycle didn't show. I went to the doctor to take a pregnancy test. The doctor came in after 10 minutes, and said, Sharon, you're pregnant. Tears began to run down my eyes. He asked me if I was okay. I answered, "No". I was disappointed, because I had been taking birth control pills to prevent getting pregnant. I told the doctor it was impossible for me to be pregnant, because I had been on birth control pills for over 6 months. He asked me if I had taken them every day on time. After little thought, I recalled my miss taking my pill one day, but I double up the next day. I thought by doubling up on the next day I would be safe and wouldn't get pregnant. The doctor told me that's why I was pregnant. He went on to say to avoid getting pregnant I should have taken the pills every morning at the same time. I told him thanks, but his advice was too late. My life took a drastic turn. I was confused, not knowing what to do, or who to tell. I had fallen into the same trap mom had fallen into at the early age of 16. Pregnant!

I was scared and tried to think of ways to tell my dad and stepmother; I had made the mistake of getting pregnant. I was sad that I had broken my promise. I kept my pregnancy a secret until I graduated - I was determined not to disappoint them.

I came home; mom was in the kitchen cooking. I said, "Mom I have something to talk to you about." She immediately stopped and sat down. I contemplated whether I should tell her. I kept hesitating whether to say something or not. Mom looked at me as if she wasn't going to move until I told her what it was I wanted to talk to her about. I finally found the courage to say, "Mom, I'm pregnant".

She turned around with a shocking and disappointing look on her face. Tears began to drop from my eyes. I was so disappointed in myself. The very thing I said, I wasn't going to do; had happened to me. I couldn't blame anyone, because no one made me have sex. I did it. I had to take full responsibility for my action. Many questions ran through my head that evening. One question I asked myself, was how in the world could I let my dad and Margaret down? I had broken my promise to them; I wasn't a good girl. I was scared; I was going to be a single parent, because the both of us was much too young to marry. The thoughts of being a single parent brought tears to my eyes. Mom looked at me, and assured me that we would work it out. She said abortion wasn't an option. She was very supportive and assured me she would help me to raise my baby, so that I could continue to go to both schools, and work. She put her arms around me, and said I know how you feel.

I appreciated mom, because she encouraged me to continue school, and graduate from the 12th grade. I took on two jobs. I worked for the 7/11 store around the corner from mom's house, and I worked a part-time job at Burger King while I furthered my clerical, computer and accounting education. It wasn't easy working two jobs, going to College and being a mother, but I managed it.

Mom watched my baby while I went to work and school. Our next-door neighbor helped us at times. I was concern about mom watching the baby, but it was something about him that brought joy to her. She slowed down on her drinking. When I told his father I had gotten pregnant, he was also disappointed. He said, he was sure I was on the pill. I told him I was and explained what could have happened. He didn't know what to do, because he too was not expecting that.

SEX FOR SALE

The man I worked for at Burger King reminded me of those dirty old men that came around mom, and great-grandmother when I was younger. Those days were over. I was old enough to protect myself from abuse and ready to beat the mess out of anyone that disrespected me. He offered the younger girls $50.00 to meet with him after work. He offered the older girls a few dollars more, and a ride on his yacht. When he approached me I told him, I wasn't interested in riding on his yacht - I was interested in owning his yacht, but he had a wife, so that wasn't an option. He was persistent at harassing us. I regretted going to work; he made our job a living hell. I had to find a way to stop him from sexually harassing us because even though we asked him to stop, he wouldn't listen.

Mom told me the importance of setting standards and not compromising my body for money. She told me it wasn't worth it. I told her she didn't have to worry; I would never belittle myself like that. I thought to myself even if I did it wouldn't be for someone as cheap as he was. It would take much more than $50.00 for me to sell my soul. Mom had shared her stories with me about the consequences of playing games on men to get their money. She shared stories with me about how men also played games on her to get sex. I asked her about the time she had come home a bloody mess. She admitted she had done some offer things. She admitted that a lot of her poor decisions were based on her using the drugs and drinking. Mom said using drugs and excessively drinking made her make some foolish decisions. She said, she was out of her mind. Mom told me never to let anyone give me drugs. I promised her I wouldn't.

I didn't want anything from him other than my paycheck, and I had earned that. I told him I was going to report him for sexual harassment if he continued to approach me. He thought I was playing so he wouldn't stop. I went to E.E.O.C. and filed a sexual harassment complaint. I was on my way to work when I ran over a nail, and my tire went flat. I was a block away from work. I called him to let him know I was on a flat up the streets from the job, and informed him I would be late. He arrogantly told me to fix the flat, and report to work. When I got there, he asked did I have any complaints, and I told him none that weren't being handled. He told me to go home that evening. I went to E.E.O.C. the next day where they followed up for several weeks, and made him give me back-pay, and my job back. I picked up my check, but I turn down his offer to work for him again. I made my point and stopped him from harassing the other ladies that worked for him. A few years later I saw his wife. She looked different. She didn't look worried; her hair was flowing, and she was smiling. I went over and spoke to her. I asked her, "How is your husband?" she said, "Your guess is as good as mine". Then she said, I don't have a clue", I divorced him." We both laughed, said our good byes and I went on my way.

Mom told me two jobs were too much for me; she said I needed to quit one and concentrate on my education. I listen, I kept the job at the Seven Eleven corner grocery, and never thought about returning to the restaurant, Burger King. The owner at Seven Eleven corner grocery store taught me a lot. He was a family man. He was married, with two daughters, and a son. Working for him was pleasant. He allowed me to make suggestions and do my job without harassing me. My responsibilities included counting inventory, re-stocking the store, running the cash register and providing the customers with good customer service. He let me work overtime to help compensate for the hours I lost at my other job. I continued going to college, and graduated. I was happy, and my parents were proud. Years later I saw the owner of the store, Burger King, his health wasn't good. He was cooking barbeque on a food truck. He spoke to me, and I spoke back. He apologizes for being nasty. I forgave him. Months later I learned that he died.

LURED INTO A TRAP

My sister met a guy that she thought was nice. They got pregnant with their first daughter. She married him and moved to California. She shared with me that she wasn't happy. She told me that she had fallen into a trap, like the trap mom had fallen into when she was young. She said, dad had left her behind in Memphis, and she didn't find mom until 6 months later." She said, "I had no place to live, so I slipped inside an old mechanic shop and slept at night. I was desperate for food, clothing and a place to sleep." She talked about how nice the guy appeared and how he promised to take care of her, only to be lured into a trap of domestic violence, drugs, alcohol, and prostitution. She said, "He drank and used drugs." I asked her "Why did you go with him." She replied, "I went because, I had no place to go. She replied, I felled into the hands of a dangerous man with hidden agendas and deadly motives.

DARK FAMILY SECRETS

As we continued to talk I thought about the night I received that call from my sister. I remembered her asking me if I could keep a secret and not to tell mom that she was being abused. I told her I would, but I didn't keep the secret, I was worried about her. I told mom, and she called Jackie and told her to bring the baby home until she got herself together. Jackie brought the baby home. She was a chocolate little girl, 10 months old.

I was the co-captain of my school cheerleader squad. It made me feel special and important to be a part of the team. I stayed active. I was a part of the cheerleader's team, the honor society group, the modern dance team and the majorettes. I felt a sense of validation, because we were required to have good grades and excellent conduct. I felt important. Mom said I had to help with my sister baby, and unless she could go to the games with me I couldn't continue to cheer. I talked to my cheerleader instructor, and told her what was going on, she made my niece a mascot so that I could continue to cheer. They even made her a little outfit like ours. I cheered until I was 6 months pregnant, and I took my niece with me to all the games. It didn't matter what we were going through we were taught to stay together and to help one another and we did.

My son was born shortly after my niece arrived in Memphis. The grandchildren made mom happy. It seemed that mom felt she was being redeemed of her sins by taking care of her grandchildren. They gave her a reason to work hard at staying sober, and making good decisions to better herself.

PEACE AT THE WATER

Mom started fishing. She said, she found peace going to the water. She said, she would go to the water and talk to God about her problems. She said, she wanted to overcome the pain she had held inside so long. She talked about how she blamed everyone for her problems when truly she needed to work on herself. She said she learned to meditate while out on the boat. She said she found peace in the water. She said she often returned to the water to ask questions.

I had purchased myself an old blue Oldsmobile to get around in. The front seats were propped up with bricks, but it got us where we needed to go. Mom would occasionally go out on a binge, but she wasn't drinking as much.

My sister decided to separate from her abusive husband, and told us she was coming home. To our surprise when she arrived, she was pregnant with her second child. We both registered to attend a clerical school called Marshall Business College to further our education. It was fun. We both completed courses in clerical, short hand and filing.

FROM BOYS TO MEN

Craig and Oliviodale continued to live with dad in Chicago, while my sister and I stayed with mom in Memphis. Dad was concern about the boys sneaking their girlfriends in the basement. He suggested they get their own apartment. Dad gave them a thirty-day notice to move. He helped them to find their own apartment, paid the deposit, first month rent and wished them well. They were angry at dad for a period. They said, dad, told them he was making men out of them by putting them out. Olivodale said, dad was making them homeless.

Olivodale laughed as we all talked about that day. They weren't given a choice; dad told them it was time to stand up and be men.

The cycle of teenage pregnancy repeated with Craig and Olivodale. Craig was a teenager when he got his first girlfriend pregnant. He was in the 12th grade. They lost contact, and he never got to know the baby. Dad told both of the boys if they were going to have children they needed to take care of them. He was upset that Craig never found his first daughter. He told them both; they needed to marry before having children. Dad explained the importance of a child needing their father. He explained how hard it was for him to be in two places at one time. He talked about how he wished mom and him would have stayed married. He said he realized how hard it was to raise children as a single parent once they divorced. He suggested to them both that before having children consider marriage so that the children would have both parents in their lives to help guide them. Craig and Olivodale listened to dad but did just the opposite of what dad told them to do. Craig broke up with his first baby momma and began dating a girl named Honey. They got pregnant. Craig said he married her after he learned she was pregnant. He wanted to do as dad told him. However, dad said marry before getting the girls pregnant. Craig said, she was a fighter, and she was verbally abusive. Craig said, he wished dad would have talked to him about women and their personalities. We laughed as we continue to talk about women fighting and being abusive. I told Craig, mom should have taught you everything you needed to know about that. Craig, laughed and agreed. Craig was a lot like dad; he never put his hands on a woman. Honey and Craig had a little girl and named her Nina. Five years later Honey died from the disease lupus. It was a sad day for Craig. Nina was taken away from him by her grandmother. Craig did all he could to have a relationship with Nina, but her grandmother wouldn't let him come around.

Years later Craig remarried and started a new family. Nina and Marissa were in Chicago. I often wondered about those girls. Wondering where were they and how were they doing. Losing contact with some of the children was painful. It reminded me of when mom told us regardless of what we go through stick together. We did. I will never forget the day we were at the florist shop; we received a call from a young lady that said she was looking for Craig Cole. She went on to ask me if I knew of a Nina Cole. I told her I thought my brother had a daughter by that name. She asked did we ever live in Chicago. I answered, yes. After we talked a little while longer, there was no doubt in my mind that she was my niece, Nina. We both were very happy that we had reconnected after 13 years. She was only 5 when her mother died. I knew my brother would be excited to hear the news. I took down her number and promised to have her father call her back immediately. When Craig returned, I gave him the exciting news. I could see the joy come across his face. We made preparation to send for her. She boarded the plane and came home to Memphis. We were all there and excited to pick her up. We could tell she was his daughter. She looked just like him. When Nina arrived, we could see the joy on her face to reconnect with her dad. I never had to experience not seeing dad for 13 years and couldn't imagine how she had been feeling all those years left alone with her grandmother. I realized that my situation wasn't as bad as Nina's. Nina had lost her mother and father. Though her father wasn't dead the pain of knowing he was alive but not being able to be with him, I would have thought was equally painful. It was beautiful to see them reunite. Craig and Nina left to go to his home to meet the rest of his family.

Unfortunately, things didn't go as we all planned. Craig wife and Nina couldn't get alone. Another situation I was all so familiar with. Nina came to stay with me. Nina wanted the attention she had missed from her father those 13 years. Craig had 4 other children at the time. His wife and Nina never bonded. I told Nina to do all she could to make her happy. It didn't work. She tried cleaning, she tried helping with the other children, she tried communicating, but none of it worked. It all reminded me of my cruel stepmother. I told Nina to pack her clothes and come stay with me for a while, hoping and praying that I could be the bridge that would help them all come together. I took her everywhere with me. We went horseback riding, swimming, to the movies, out of town, shopping, in the park and over to moms to talk to her about her feelings. I will never forget recording Nina singing a song called it's over now, the storm is over now. The chorus went, I feel like I can make it the storm is over now. No more crying days they are gone away, I feel like

I can make it the storm is over now. She sang it beautifully. Nina made her rounds visiting everyone. She spent time getting to know her Uncle Olivodale, he said, he enjoyed her staying with him, because he got a chance to know his niece but living in a rooming house wasn't a place for a girl, so he told her to go spend time with Jackie. She went to visit with Jackie and her girls for a short period and then returned to her father's house. After trying once again, Nina went back to Chicago. I was grateful for the months we shared together, we had a chance to talk about a lot of her childhood memories. It hurt to see her leave.

One night while in my floral shop working on a wedding, the telephone rung. I answered. It was a call from Chicago Illinois. On the other end was a relative of Nina's, the lady asked to speak to Craig, I told her he wasn't in, but I was his sister. She went on to say that she was sad to give me bad news but, Nina had committed suicide. My heart dropped, the phone got silent. Tears began to fall down my eyes. I didn't know what to think. There was nothing more I could do but drop to my knees and cry. I regretted sharing the news with Craig, but I did, and we all packed our things and went to Chicago to bury Nina. It was sad to witness how cold step parents were. I had a flashback of when Olivodale like many times before suggested we go handle our business. And like before I gathered my little self, got in the car and headed over to my brother's Craig's house to have a talk about Nina. The stepmother talked a lot of mess, and before I knew it, I was whipping her like I would have that selfish stepmother of mine. My dad came running around the corner, he was upset. He told Olivodale and me we were wrong. There were times I found myself in a place where it wasn't right, but I didn't want to see Nina be hurt. I surely didn't want her to commit suicide. Nina wanted love from her father. It was a sad day for us all. Nina was gone, and the baby was too. You see when we arrived at the hospital we were told that Nina was pregnant. We weren't sure why she committed suicide but two things we learned was she was looking for love from her father and from her relationship. I don't think her void was ever fulfilled so she put the gun up to her head and shot herself. Craig was left grieving. He said all he was left with was a note.

Oliviodale was a teenager in the 11th grade when he got two girls pregnant at the same time. He said, he was going to be the best father he could to his children, but the marriage wasn't what he wanted to do. We laughed as we talked about having children and getting married. I told Olivodale I knew marriage wasn't for him because he couldn't marry two girls at one time. He agreed. He later had two other children by another girl and then another two children by another. It was clear he was doing things his way because he did nothing dad told him when it came to having children. Olivodale did what he could to keep a relationship going with all them, but being so young he lost contact with two of the children. Later Olivodale struggle with alcohol and some of the same cycles we went through began to fall upon his children. Dad explained to Olivodale that the worst thing a man could do is leave his children behind. Dad always told the boys if they had children it was their responsibility to raise them. I later learned it was more than just our responsibility to raise them, but it was our responsibility to guide them. I found that to guide them we had to get ourselves together first. Olivodale ended up with 6 children.

We all did our best to take care of our children but, because we were young teenage children having children our best wasn't good enough. The cycle of teenage pregnancy was traveling from one generation to another hurting the children in our families. Some of the children were caught up in the government system, while others suffered from being raised in a single parent household. Everyone was suffering from lack of knowledge. There was nothing I could do, but work on stopping the cycles. There was plenty of work to do in our family to stop the many dysfunctional behaviors from constantly traveling through our family. The first thing I felt we needed to do was, to tell the truth, the whole truth and not but the truth about the things that we as children had experienced. Perhaps this would teach our children to avoid the traps that were set for us.

IF A MAN HIT YOU ONCE
HE WILL HIT YOU AGAIN

My sister stayed in Memphis for a little while. She said, she didn't want to deal with mom and her men fighting. She returned to California to make it work with her husband. She hoped he had changed. He said he wasn't pimping women any longer and promised never to hit her again. He was in school studying to be a professor. She wanted so badly to break the cycle of single parenting. She did all she could to stay married to the children father, but the abuse didn't stop.

We both remembered the old people and great-grandma saying, it was better to be married than to be a fornicator or adulteress woman. Great-grandmother often said, "spare the rod spoil the child" my sister believed in disciplining her children. She said, she wanted them to be successful, and by whipping them, she felt it would make them successful. After her fourth child; she saw that her husband abusive drug and alcoholic ways weren't going to change, so she separated from him, again. She started her life as a single parent and did the best she could to raise her four children. Jackie said, she learned to trust God. She started spending most of her time reading the Bible, and getting to know more about God. She said, she learned that God did love her, in- spite of what great-grandmother had to say.

Single parenting was another cycle that was running rapid in our family. The boys were single, and the girls were single. Mom told us that being single raising children made life hard for her.

I started my life as a young teenage girl, and mother at the early teenage of 17. I was obviously raised in two different environments, because I lived with both my mother and my father. My father household was functional and my mother household chaotic and dysfunctional. I chose whether I would live a functional or dysfunctional lifestyle. I choose functional. I learned from my mother bad life experiences and worked hard at breaking the cycles of bad habits and behavior. Mom showed me what a lifestyle of single parenting, alcoholism, drugs and domestic violence felt like. Dad showed me how a functional lifestyle felt.

Though he had selfish women in his life at times, his environment was peaceful once he found the right soul mate. He worked and stayed sober. He occasionally had a sociable drink, but never did I see him drunk. I took the good and the bad experiences from both of my parents and used them to help re-create myself by stopping the dysfunctional cycles from repeating in and through my life.

SETTING STANDARDS

I began setting standards based on the good and the bad I learned from both my parents. I made a vow to myself that I would never date a man that verbally, physically or mentally abuse me. I made another vow to never tolerate or settle for a relationship that was drug or alcohol driven. I was taught from living with mom and her men friends that alcohol and drugs contributed to her chaotic environment.

I told mom I would be moving soon, and began to prepare myself. She felt sad at first but, when I told her I was moving two doors down from her house, she felt better about my move. I purchased the small things first, towels, knives, spoons, sheets, curtains, bedroom furniture, and a table set. I paid on the rest of my furniture until I paid it off and then had it delivered to my place. I was excited to start a life of my own. Once I finish paying off my furniture bill, I made my deposit, paid my first month rent, and schedule my move in date. When I moved, I asked mom if she would keep my sign on my bedroom door. I told her I wanted the sign to remain just in case I needed to come back. The sign read "Sharon's Room." My place was a nice duplex apartment, with two bedrooms, a front room, dining room, kitchen, and large fenced in back and front yard. Mom was happy for me and like before, encouraged me to move forward.

I knew 17 was young for a girl to leave home, but I took the risk, my son was one-year-old. I wanted to raise my child in a better environment. I didn't want him to be exposed to the many dysfunctional behaviors I had been exposed to. I wanted to make sure I protected him, and exposed him to a safe, secure environment. I didn't allow strangers to hold him or baby sit him. I didn't trust people with him. I was grateful to have my mother as my support system.

I accepted the mistake of getting pregnant too young and had to deal with the consequences. I dealt with those things I could change and accepted the ones that I couldn't. I love my son, and he brought me joy, the rest I said I would take one day at a time and I did.

I spent time reading the Bible and studying my school work. I knew I had a calling on my life; I just didn't know what I was called to do. I meet a nice gentleman that worked for a lady's shoe store in East Memphis. I told him I was abstaining from sex.

He said he didn't have a problem with it. He shared with me that he had been separated from his wife over 5 years and they were going through a divorce. I was taught by great-grandmother that if I slept with a married man, I would be an adulteress woman.

We both liked each other enough to wait before having sex. Mom taught me to give all things Godly consideration before moving forward with my decisions. After carefully thinking about my decisions to be his friend, I began to feel guilty, because he was still married. I told him I thought it might be best for him to get divorced before we continued our friendship. He was heartbroken.

He made a promise that he wouldn't cross the line. I told him I wasn't worried about him crossing the line, I was worried about me. We laughed with one another and decided that we would be friends, but we wouldn't move forward into a relationship until his divorce was final. We began to study the Bible together. He had a little girl the same age, my son. One day he brought her over for us to meet. The two of the children got along well. We often took the two of the children out on dates with us. The more we studied the Bible and spent time with our children, I could see the possibilities of being a family. I felt myself falling in love with him. We had so much fun together. We went to the movies together, rode horses, and took road trips to Nashville, Alabama and other places near for the weekends. We were best friends. We often purchased and wore matching clothes. There wasn't a day that he didn't call and check on me and my son. We continued to go to church and study our Bible together.

DOES HE WANT HER OR ME?

One night he called, and told me he needed to talk to me, but he didn't want to talk over the telephone. I got excited. I immediately started to ask what it was. He wouldn't tell me. I knew it had to be related to the divorce. I knew he was possibly going to tell me the divorce was final, and he wanted to marry me. Tears gathered in my eyes. Then I drifted off thinking maybe he was going to go back to his wife. I was nervous. Either one was going to be hard for me. If he asked me to marry him, I would have to say no, because honestly, I wasn't ready, but if he said he was going back to his wife my heart was going to be crushed. I got dressed and waited for him to show.

I waited and waited and waited for him to show, but he didn't. It got to be around 10 pm. I got worried. I didn't want to call him, because after not hearing from him I was afraid to hear what he had to say. It was unlike him not to call and cancel a date; I forced myself to call him. The telephone rung six times, and then it went to voicemail. No answer. I waited an hour, and called again, and still, I got no answer. It was late. I went to check on my baby boy, he was sleep and resting well. I had been waiting all day for him to come, but after the clock struck 12midnight, I took off my clothes put on my night clothes and went to bed. The next morning about 6 am my phone rung. I answered. It was him on the other line. I asked, "Are you okay?" He said. "No, I'm not doing well at all," I asked what's wrong? "He asked, is it too early to come over?" I asked, "Where are you coming from?" He said, "I'm on my way." I asked again, "Where are you coming from"? He said, "Open the door, I'll be there in a moment." I asked, Are you sure? He said quietly, "Yes."

In about 10 minutes he was knocking on the door. He tried to hug me, but I asked again, "Where are you coming from, and why couldn't you answer my calls last night?" He said, "I regret telling you this" tears began to run down my eyes, he said, "I was at my wife's house." My heart dropped, and my eyebrows raised. He said, "We had a long talk, and I feel compelled to try to make the relationship work with her for the sake of our daughter." I said, "Let me make this clear, did you say your wife?" He said, "Yes". I stood there in shock and said after five years. He said, "I'm so sorry." I opened the door and told him to leave. I needed to get myself together. He walked out with his head hanging. I felt like he had stabbed me in my stomach with a knife. I couldn't eat for weeks. He called, but I wouldn't take the calls. I had compromised my beliefs, and I was suffering the consequences of falling in love with a married man.

Mom said, if I ever needed to get over a person, find a song to sing and sing it until I got tired of the song - I needed a song. Mom said by the time I got tired of singing the song I would be over the relationship. I found a song, and sung it until I got tired of the song. Each day I waited for his phone call, each night I waited to get the phone call from him to say goodnight. I was lost for a while. I missed my friend. I accepted he wasn't mine and moved forward.

Mom and Marcus downsized, and moved to the projects - Fowler Homes. There lived a lady next door to mom named Mrs. Helen who helped my mother, and I with my baby. She was the only person I trusted to help us. I made sure he could talk before trusting someone else to help us with him. She bathe him, kept him clean, and fed him, while I worked and went to college. She reminded me of my great-grandmother, because she went to church Sunday, Monday, Tuesday, Wednesday, Thursday, Friday, and Saturday. She was strict, but I trusted her with my son, because when I got there to pick him up, he was dry, clean, fed and would always be smiling.

DEPRESSION

Oliviodale was working as a mechanic in Chicago, and had started a family with not one, but two girls. One of his girlfriends called to tell us he had threatened to commit suicide. She said, he was using drugs and had become depressed. Jackie was back in Memphis visiting and suggested we go and see about him. We boarded the plane to Chicago, while mom talked to him on the telephone until we arrived. When we landed, we caught a cab, and went straight to him. He was shocked to see us, but one thing we all knew to do is stick together regardless of our circumstances. All we had was each other growing up as children. We brought Oliviodale back home to momma. They had a long talk about the use of drugs and falling into depression. He stayed for a week and returned to Chicago, packed his things, and he and his girlfriend moved to Memphis with their babies.

NO MORE FIGHTING

I told Oliviodale about mom and her drinking and fighting. The next day we returned to visit our mother. Marcus and mom had gotten into another bad fight. Mom asked Marcus to leave; she said she was tired of arguing and fighting. He pointed his finger at mom's face, and mom cut his finger almost off. Mom's face was busted, her mouth was swollen, and her eye was blackened. Enough was enough and "no more" is what we said. We were older now and could help mom deal with her abusive men. Olivodale and I went to purchase a gun. We were teenagers; we were going to shoot him. We hadn't considered the consequences. I knew a guy in the neighborhood that sold guns. We went to him gave him $50.00 to purchase a gun. He told me the gun had 6 bullets in it and was already loaded. Olivodale and I went to mom's house, and hid behind the tree in front of her apartments. We waited for Marcus to come to the apartments that evening. While waiting all I could think about is all the men that had beat my mother. I was no longer going to tolerate the abuse. When he walked up, I pulled the trigger, but nothing came out. I tried again, and still, nothing came out. Oliviodale and I kept that as a secret for a long time. We didn't tell anyone what we had plotted until later when we shared it with our siblings, Craig, and Jackie. The gun that we purchase was no good. It was stopped up with steel. I realized it was a blessing that the gun was stopped up with steel, because we would have been in jail. The jail wasn't somewhere I wanted to visit.

The next day we went over to visit with mom to tell her what we had plotted, she wasn't home, but Marcus was. When he answered the door, I asked if my mother was home he said, "No." I asked him if he could come out on the porch, and talk to me. He looked at me strangely, but he came out. He took a seat on the porch. I told him that I had seen my mother be abused, and live in a dysfunctional relationship most of my life and I needed him to promise me one thing. He asked what? My brother walked around the corner with a baseball bat in his hands. I continue to say, "Please keep your hands off my mother." He looked at me, and started to say something. I stopped him and asked, "Do you have a mother?" He said, "She's dead." I asked him, "How did she die?"

He said, "I don't know. We never had a relationship." I could see why he didn't know how to treat a woman, because his mother wasn't in his life. He looked at us and told us he would never put his hands on our mother again. Olivodale looked at him with a killer look on his face and said nothing. I thanked him, and left. I called mom later that night, and asked what was she doing she said, "I'm helping Marcus to move his things out". I asked. "Is everything okay?" She said, "Yes actually it is." I smiled.

DON'T COMPETE
FOR LOVE

Oliviodale and I fought together. It never mattered who was right or wrong; if Oliviodale said we needed to fight, it was on. Though it appeared that mom favored her girl's children, she loved all her grandchildren. She bonded with the girl's children because, once we all separated the girls came back to Memphis to be with mom, while the boys remained in Chicago to be with dad. Jackie and my children were in Memphis with us, so mom saw a lot of them. The boy's children were in Chicago with Dad, and Margaret. They spent more time with our dad, and stepmother. Later once the boys returned to Memphis they had more children, and they all grew up around mom. Mom loved them all the same. She had her way of making them compete. If one of the grandchildren brought her a gift, she called the other ones and bragged. She caused the other grandchildren to compete with gifts. Some of the grandchildren grew up thinking that they had to buy love. Others grew up thinking they were never good enough. Mom teaching the children to compete for her love caused some of the grandchildren to look for validation from others by competing constantly with one another. We had to later teach some of the grandchildren that they didn't have to compete for love, and that it was okay for all of them to be praised according to their individual progress, behavior, gifts, and accomplishments. Some got it, while some didn't.

Marcus gathered his things and went on his way. Mom seemed to be co-dependent and had to have a man in her life because once Marcus left, mom got with this guy named Buddy. It seemed like mom always found another man to get over the other man. She would get out of one bad situation, and go immediately into another one. I asked mom one day, why she dated men that were abusive. Mom admitted she never had a relationship with her father and she didn't know what to expect from men. Mom continued drinking and hanging out. She married while she was intoxicated. She was 42 years old. She said, she went to sleep intoxicated, and when she woke up, she realized she was married. They went to the courthouse and married. She said, she wanted so badly to get out of the marriage, but it was too late. She said, she had fallen into another trap. She had made a drunken decision. Buddy appeared to be a nice person, but he was an alcoholic like the other men, and the cycle repeated itself. They started to fight and argue. Mom could say things out of her mouth that cut like a knife, and she didn't fight fair. She said, there was nothing about fighting fair. She became a violent lady and verbally abusive. Many times, mom provoked the fights, and the outcome was a bloody mess. She said, she took her anger out on him for all the abusive men she had ever met. She said, he made her hate men so much she would rather have been with a woman.

Mom was searching for love; she cried when she talked about never finding her father, and having a relationship with her mother. She felt she wasn't good enough. The men she was attracted to didn't know what to give because they had not been loved by a mother or father themselves. Mom was attracting men that raised themselves. I never recalled any of those men having a mother or father in their lives. Not having parents to guide them made a big difference. I realized that I too made a bad decision when I was left alone. It was a fact that these individuals had a lot of anger locked up in the inside, and was sedating it with drugs, and alcohol wasn't resolving the problem. We weren't living with mom any longer but, we knew she was still in domestic violent relationships because, we could look at her and tell. Mom said, she was tired of living in abusive relationships, and that this would be the last abusive relationship she would live in. Often mom would plot and premeditate doing something dirty to her men. After so much abuse in the relationship, she said one day, his happiest day was going to be his saddest day, and I feared what mom was premeditating to do to him.

Buddy left the house one evening; mom poured gasoline all around the house. Jackie ran over to the house, and asked mom what was she doing? Mom said, "Enough is enough." "I'm going to come back and set the house on fire when he comes in." Buddy didn't come in that night; my sister convinced her not to burn the house down. Mom waited for the mailman to come. Mom knew Buddy had an income tax check on the way. The mailman came, and the check was delivered. Mom took the $5000.00 check, checkbook, jewelry, big screen TV's and everything else she could get on the U-Haul. She left and never returned.

We all pitched in and got her a nicer apartment; it was enough room for her and the grandchildren when they wanted to visit. After 20 years of loneliness, crime, abuse, drugs, and alcohol, mom asked for help, and we were old enough to help her.

SEX AND WORK

I continued College. This time I was studying to be a computer operator and accountant. I graduated with the help of mom. I received a second interview at a used car lot for a bookkeeping position. I remembered when I got the job, Mr. Wallace said my background check was clean, but he had one concern. He said he learned that I had taken a former employer to E.E.O.C. and wanted to know why. I told him that my former employer offered $50.00 to young girls including myself to ride on his yacht and have sex with him. I told him, I wasn't interested in having sex with him. I shared how the employer became mean, and would sexually harass me. I asked him did he have any hidden motives. He said with hesitance in his voice, no.

Mr. Wallace hired me at a salary of $250.00 per week plus commissions. My commissions soon resulted in my checks doubling and sometimes tripling. I was making good money and living a nice lifestyle. Mom taught her girls to be independent, and never depend on anyone to supply our needs. I listen to her. I dated, but never depended on men to be responsible for my bills. I did depend on them to be gentlemen, and show me a good time, and buy me gifts periodically, and talk to me intelligently.

THE BEGINNING
TO REHAB

One-night mom asked me to come over she wanted to have a talk with me. I got off work and stopped by. She said she wanted to overcome her addiction to alcohol, drugs and abusive men, but she did not know how. She said, she was tired of the cycle. The next day I got the telephone book and started searching for help. I gathered a list of places and took the day off work to check them out. Mom and I went to several rehab centers hoping to find help. Her ex-husband and she were separated but, he was still carrying the medical insurance on her. However, we later learned that the insurance wouldn't take care of the mental care she needed. Every center we went to turned us down. We were frustrated, and close to giving up. That evening we ended our search at a Downtown Mental Health and Rehab Center. The director could see how desperate we were for help. The alternative they gave us was to pay $16,000.00 for the six-month program and be placed on a waiting list. Mom looked at me and said to me, "Come on baby, there's no way you can raise that kind of money." She looked like she was ready to be set free. I considered her eyes; she considered mine. I felt hopeless, because mom was sad.

I had no idea how I would come up with so much money, but I knew I had to get my mother help. We thanked him for his help, I gave him my phone number and left. He took our information, and said if he came up with something he would call me. We got in my car and headed to the house. I left mom at her house and went to mine. That night I pondered how to get mom help, she went on a binged and left that night, and to the streets, she went, I couldn't find her for several weeks. I worried about her. I told my brothers I couldn't find mom. My sister was back on the road; she had relocated to Houston, Texas. I was lonely. My siblings weren't there to help me. Never had I been faced alone with such a task this big.

THAT'S MY MOTHER

I went to work late; my co-workers were laughing and talking about this lady that had come on the car-lot drunk. They talked about her dirty clothes and how she was staggering. I was laughing as they continued to describe her behavior. The lady was still outside. As she continues to stagger towards the office – about to fall, I told my co-workers we needed to give the lady some crutches. The closer she got to us, the clearer her face became. It was my mother! I was embarrassed.

I walked outside, asked mom what was wrong; she said she needed money. Mom was out of control! I went back into the office and told the crew I needed to leave. One of the guys asked why? I dropped my head, as I left and said I need to go get my mother some help. The crew was shocked and apologized. I convinced mom to get in my car, and we drove off. Mom wanted money to get more to drink. As I drove, she threatened to jump out. She wanted something to drink. Traffic was heavy - I was doing all I could to prevent wrecking the car. I managed to keep her in the car long enough to drive to the nearest place I could get immediate help. That place ends up being at a mental institute. I didn't know it was for mentally disturbed people, all I knew was mom needed help. As I drove up to the institute, I asked one of the security guards to get help. He helped me to get mom out of the car and into the building. The doctors admitted mom and sedated her to calm her down, because she was in a rage. I cried, and pleaded with them not to hurt my mother. They kept her for two weeks for evaluation and to detox her. Meanwhile, I called several rehab facilities before returning to work but still no success. It was late when I returned to work my boss, was there, the crew had left for the evening.

Mr. Wallace said the crew told him I left with my mother because she was drunk. He asked me was I, okay, I replied, "No." He began to tell me a story about his alcohol addiction back in his earlier days, and how he struggled to overcome his addition.

DESPERATE AND COMPROMISED

I was vulnerable to help that night. Mr. Wallace asked what facility I had taken her. I told him to The Downtown Mental Institute. I explained that everybody wanted cash up front. Mr. Wallace said he would help me. I could feel, it was going to cause me compromising my morals. The very thing I said I would never do. I felt horrible to be considering compromising my body for money. I thought about all the time's mom, and her friends had traded their bodies for money. I knew mom would have not wanted me to repeat the cycle of prostitution, but I was desperate.

I knew better, after all, I had vowed to break dysfunctional cycles. My first mind said don't do it. My second mind reminded me that my mom needed help. I tossed and turned that night trying to decide. I knew what I was about to do was wrong, but I convinced myself that I would be doing it for a good reason. I was doing it to help my mother. I promised that I would do it one time and never again - $16,000 were a lot of money. I wasn't worried about him asking too to see me often. I asked God, for forgiveness before I met him at the hotel the next day. I had a flashback as I drove towards the hotel room where I remembered mom, and her friends doing drugs, plotting sex scandals. I thought about the time's mom met guys at the hotel, put something in their drink, and took their money then left. Most times when the men caught up with her, it ends in a deadly fight. I could imagine how desperate mom felt. I went into the room and quickly closed the door.

I was seventeen. It felt nasty. He touched me. I wanted to get it over with. This was so degrading to me. I had a flashback it reminded me of when I was the innocent age of 10. He too didn't do anything but lick me. I was glad it didn't take long. When he finished, he gave me the $16,000 cashier's check and asked was I okay? As I took the check, I cried and said, "No". As I proceeded towards the door, I looked around before getting into my car praying that no one saw me as I was leaving the hotel. I saw a black maid getting ready to go into one of the rooms to clean it. I felt ashamed as I passed her, because I felt she knew what I had done. I knew he wouldn't ask to see me again anytime soon, and I knew that I could now get my mother some help. I took the check to the bank. I shared it with a friend. My friend joked about it and asked me was it $1600.00, because no black guy was going to give me that kind of money. I told him he wasn't a black guy, and yes, he did give me $16,000.00. There were other girls that used older men for their needs. However, they called them their sugar daddy. I had no intention of having a sugar daddy and nor was I going to repeat the cycle of prostitution. I could tell mom everything, but this was one thing I said I would never share. I knew it would break her heart if she thought I did such. I didn't tell anyone in fear the word would get back to her. I kept my own secret.

HELP PLEASE

A few days later I received a call from The Downtown Mental Institute, the doctor told me they were going to release mom, and I could come pick her up. When I arrived to pick her up, she was angry, and said some hurtful things to me. She said she hated me; she called me bitches, whores and all kinds of names. She threw her shoes at me, and told me to leave. She was upset that I had admitted her to the mental institute. I explained to her that I had no other choices. I explained how out of control she was. Once I told her she tried to jump out the car into the ongoing traffic. She quietens down, gathered her things, and we left together. Keep in mind I was only seventeen. I didn't know many seventeen-year-old girls that were faced with the challenge of helping their mom's overcome drugs, and alcohol, but I was, and I did what I had to do.

That night, I drove the city talking to mom, and trying to figure out what to do, I went by my apartment picked up some cash, and took mom to the liquor store to get her something to drink. It was one of the cheapest drinks they sold. It was called Mad Dog 20 - 20. Mom always said, when she was troubled she would go to the water. We had troubles that night. She said that because she didn't have her parents to guide, and teach her, she often went to the water expecting God to show up. She said, God spirit, taught her everything she knew. That night I wanted to see if God was going to meet us at the water with answers. We really needed answers, because I had no idea what to do. Mom, and I sat at the Mississippi River for hours. I had never got drunk before, but this night it was on. I needed to get to mom's level to feel what she was going through. I wanted her to tell me about those locked up childhood memories. I wanted to know if they were like mine. Mom talked about the same thing she had talked to me about before, and that was she missed her mom, and she wished her dad would have been in her life. She talked about how the drugs had caused her to lose her mine. I wanted my mother back; enough was enough. I wanted that pretty coca cola bottle, peachy color skin woman everyone told me about. I drunk the entire bottle of wine, and she drank her 20/20. We sat on the river, and talked about a lot of things. I cried, she cried. She laughed, and I laughed. We got dirty drunk together. I forgot she was my mom – we were more like sisters. We stayed at the river until 4:00 a.m. that morning talking about old times and mom's painful childhood memories. By the time we got ready to leave, mom was motivated to get help. I found myself being like her. All those times she had encouraged me when I was down, I was now encouraging her. The cycle was repeating itself, but in a good way.

We both felled asleep in the car that night. We awaken, and went back to the rehab center where we had been told it would cost $16,000.00 to get mom help. I felt bad about what I had done but, I left it in the water. Mom, and I felt and looked like crap. I asked her could we do what big momma had taught us to do, she said, "let's do it." We prayed for forgiveness, help, directions, and the will power to stop the dysfunctional cycles from repeating in our lives. We asked God to please help us stop the pain of our childhood memories. Before we ended the prayer, I said to God, please forgive me for selling my soul. Mom looked at me strangely, but she didn't get it, and I'm glad she didn't. I said let's go back to the rehab center. Mom said, "Why are we going back there? I don't have $16,000.00, and I know you don't." She said, "We're wasting time". I said nothing; I drove to the center.

RESOURCES SAVED MY MOTHER'S LIFE

I didn't remember the man's name, but as we walked into the office, he was approaching the front desk. He said Ms. Cole "I've been trying to call you, but I got no answer," he said, "Come into my office, I got your mom some help, but you have to take her to Jonesboro, Arkansas." I told him, "That would work". I knew that if mom went out of town that would keep her from getting the drugs, because she didn't know anyone in that city. This was great news for both of us. I looked at my mother as tears began to roll down her eyes, I knew she was ready. I told the man okay, and that I would be right back - I needed to go to the bank quickly. He asked, as I began to leave his office, "Why do you need to go to the bank?" He went on to say, "If you take her to Jonesboro, Arkansas it's free." Tears of joy ran down my face as mom looked at me. She said, "Let's go." We were so happy.

He told us to be back to his office by 2:00 pm that evening to fill out the paperwork. We rushed home, packed and returned to his office. Suddenly I realized that not only did we have mom some help, but I also had $16,000 that I could keep. I know God showed up at the water, because he made a bad situation good. God saw my heart. I vowed never to use my body for money again. I didn't want to fall into the trap of prostitution - I wanted help for my mother. I never told my boss, I didn't have to use the money to get mom help. Instead, I put it in the bank for a rainy day. The doctor scheduled mom to leave the next day. I called my two brothers, and told them that I had gotten mom some help. They both drove down from Chicago to ride with us. Mom was happy to see the boys. It had been a while since they had been home. Jackie couldn't be with us, but she sent her love. We filled the car with gas, and drove mom to Jonesboro, Arkansas.

As Craig drove us, I prayed that where ever we were taking mom it would be beautiful, and not in the hood or some rooming house. Mom wasn't crazy - it was those drugs that made her do the disgusting things she did. I told mom that it was a beautiful place, we drove anticipating what we would see when we got there. As we drove toward the street address, the houses in the area were getting larger, and larger. They were mansions. I couldn't believe my eyes as we pulled up to the house. There were wealthy looking women, and no men. It was set up like a bed, and breakfast facility. The women shared a front room, laundry room, kitchen, and a large TV room. The women had their own bedroom, and they had several bathrooms to share. The house had a beautiful front and backyard, full of trees, blooming plants, gazebos, and waterfalls. Mom got out of the car; her eyes lit up like a little girl. She was impressed with the house and happy to stay.

We all hugged mom and said our goodbyes. I turn around to look at mom, I saw the tears in her eyes, but I knew they were tears of joy. I finally felt like I could get some rest. I knew mom was somewhere safe and I knew she would be treated well. As we drove away, we were all happy to know that mom was finally getting help for her addiction to drugs, and alcohol. Mom's healing had begun, and meanwhile, We were all living our lives. I trusted God in all our healing. We all were glad that she wasn't on the streets drinking, drugging and fighting and that she was in a safe place receiving help. Jackie was off to herself, and often traveled with her children from Texas to California.

WORKING ON SELF

After my sister and I had shared so much of our childhood, teenage and young adult experience we decided we needed to work on ourselves. After having my bad experience with my friend that decided to go back to his wife, I decided I wouldn't date for a while. I was back to abstinence from sex. We both vowed to refrain from sex, and concentrated on raising our children. Being a single mom didn't allow me time to have a relationship. I had friends that I occasionally went to movies, on walks, and periodically to dinner. I concentrated on College, and graduated as an accountant. I kept my promise this time. I made Margaret, dad, mom and my sister proud of me.

HE WASN'T WHO
HE SAID HE WAS

    I planned to marry after graduating. I wanted a companion, and I wanted my child to be raised by a father in the home. My son and I were living in a nice duplex, and I was working making a decent salary. I envisioned the type of guy I wanted. Everything other than what my mother had experienced. If they were abusive to women, alcohol or drugs - I didn't deal with them. A guy had been visiting my neighbor's house for Bible study and had been asking her about me. She told him what she knew about me, which was very little. On several occasions, he asked me out on a date. After a few months, I accepted a date from him, and we went out. He told me good things about himself. He said, he was a single man, no children, owned his own home, two cars, made a decent salary and ministered to a small church located around the corner from my house. He said, he was looking for a wife. It was getting close to Christmas, and everybody was happy and in a giving mood. I met his family, and fell in love with his mother and sisters. Even though there wasn't a father in the house, I assumed he knew his dad. After all, he said, he knew how to provide for a woman.

    After the boys rode to Jonesboro, Arkansas with me to take mom to the rehab center, they returned to Chicago. Mom was in rehab, my sister was off in Texas raising her children as a single parent, and I was alone in Memphis. After knowing him for only two months he proposed to me, and I accepted - after all, he knew God, and he was a minister that quoted scriptures quite well. He was handsome, fair complexion, curly hair, slim and well dressed. He said he didn't use drugs, fight, drank or cuss. I felt it would be safe to marry, because of his spiritual background. I announced to my family that I was getting married. We had a large wedding. My sister traveled home, and made the girls dresses. Christen didn't give me money towards the wedding, because he said the tradition was that weddings were paid for by the girl's parents. My parents didn't have money to pay for my wedding, so I paid for it myself. I paid close to

$10,000.00 for the wedding. I was excited to pick the beautiful colorful flowers, designs, and candles. His mother was a great cook; she agreed to do the reception food.

The day of the wedding all hell broke loose. It seemed that we were running into all kind of problems. My sister said she was running out of time, and may not be able to finish the girl's dresses. A few of the girl's dresses had to be pinned on, because time had drawn near, and it was time for the ceremony to start. I was nervous as my father walked me down the aisle. The night before the wedding Christian's aunt asked me was I sure he was going to show up. I was surprised, and concerned that she would ask me something like that. As my father walked me down the aisle, I told dad, I didn't know if I had made the right decision. Dad said, "You don't have to do this, we can turn around." As I got closer to the altar, I said, "I'll give it a try." When the pastor said, who giveth this woman to be married, my father said, I do. Dad put my hands in his, and we stood before the Pastor and said vows to one another. We were married. We danced, and had fun with our relatives, and friends. Christen got drunk and went to sleep the moment we got in our hotel room. I was tired too, so many obstacles had gotten in the way that day, and I couldn't wait to shut my eyes. We both went to sleep. The next day we were off to Houston for our honeymoon.

I was excited to take the ride. We gathered our bags, jumped in the car, and off we went to Houston, Texas. I turned on the radio station when I got in the car and listen to love songs. One of my favorite songs came on, and I started dancing in my seat. Christen turned down the radio, and said we needed to talk business. He said we needed to add his name to my bank account, and I asked him, how much money did he have in his account, he replied, "$600.00" - I had $18,000.00 in my bank account. I told him I couldn't agree with adding his name to my account, but I had no problem opening a joint account together. He asked me, "Why do you have a problem with my name going on your bank account?" He said, "We're married now, and your money is my money, and my money is your money".

I said, "But you don't have any money". He said, shut up, and listen while I'm talking". I frowned. He went on to say, "We don't need a sports car, so we're going to trade in your two-seater sports car for a family car." He said, "We need a Cadillac." I told him, "I don't need a Cadillac, I like my sports car." I told him my car had enough room for me, and my son. I then suggested that he keep his car, and I keep mine. He got angry, and start shouting at me. He said, "You don't have a voice in this family, you will do as I say from now on." He went on to say there were going to be some changes made, and he would make all the business decisions going forth. I knew then; I had a problem. When we arrived at his family's house, I faked like everything was cool in front of his cousins, but in the inside, I was boiling with anger, I couldn't wait to get back to

Memphis. I knew once we got back the marriage would be over. I was going to my attorney's office and file for an annulment. I didn't want to be married to him.

We stayed with his cousins for the weekend. I tried to enjoy myself, but it was hard, all I kept thinking about is the man thinks I'm trading my car and adding his name to my bank account. I felt tricked. We didn't consummate the wedding. On the way back, the conversation started again. I told him, "I'm not going to add my money with yours, and neither am I going to trade my car for a Cadillac. The next thing I knew his hand came across my face. He backhanded slapped me. I was shocked, frighten and scared. I didn't know what to do. I called him a "Mother Fucker." He grabbed me by my hair, and held my head down. I screamed, "Let me out - let me out of this car." He pulled over to the side of the road, and beat me in my head. I kept screaming until he let go of my hair and stop hitting me. He wouldn't let me out of the car. I was a long way from home, so I didn't attempt to jump. I rode back to Memphis, not saying a word. I was quiet for over 8 hours. It took everything I had in me to shut up. Tears of rage and anger ran down my cheeks. I said to myself, your happiest day will be your saddest day ever. I remembered momma saying those words. After seeing my mother be abused by so many men I promised that I would never tolerate a domestic violent relationship. This was another vow that I was going to keep. The cycle of domestic violence stopped with me. I couldn't wait to get back to Memphis; he had put his hands on the wrong person. I had all kinds of thoughts running through my head.

My first stop was going to be to my attorney's office; the marriage was over.

THE CYCLE OF DOMESTIC VIOLENCE STOP WITH ME

When we arrived in Memphis, I asked him to pack his things, and leave. He left, but he didn't take his clothes. The next morning, I called my attorney, and told him I wanted the marriage annulled. I told him what happened during the 5 days we had been married. My attorney told me to come to his office the next day.

The next day I went in to further discuss the lies he used to lure me in to the marriage and the abuse he thought he could use to control me. After talking to my attorney, he agreed that I should file for a divorce. I told him, I didn't want a divorce, because I had only been married 5 days, I wanted the marriage annulled and voided. What he didn't know is the cycle of fighting had transferred on to me, but the cycle of accepting abuse had not. My attorney drafted the paperwork, and I signed it. I realized it was getting close to the time for me to pick my son up from School and I quickly signed the papers, said my goodbyes and off I went. When I got to the school, the principal said they had called the house to see where I was, because my husband was there to pick up my son. They said since his name was on the form they let him leave with him. I was scared, I rushed to my car, drove to my house as fast as I could. I pulled up in my drive, and his car was in the driveway. I walked in the house, and heard my son screaming. I rushed to the back bathroom to see what was going on, he pushed me away, and said I'll handle this. He said my son had stolen 50 cents off the dresser. My son was accustomed to getting change off the dresser, because that's where I left change for him. He made my son go to bed early that night, and threatened me not to go into his room. I asked him why he was back. He said, everything I own was his now. I counted to ten to keep from throwing a bottle at him. I didn't want to scare my son any more than he had already done. So, I premeditated what would be next.

Christen left early the next day for work. I got up, went to my son's room to dress him for school, and found whips on his body. His eye was bruised. I got my pistol, and went to his mother's house. I expected to see him, but he wasn't there. I showed his mother the bruises on my child, and let her feel the knots in my head where he had beaten me on the way back to Memphis in the car. She was sad, but there was nothing she could do, but shake her head. She was disgusted. I could see the disappointment on her face. She grabbed me and cried.

I went back home that evening, changed my locks, and threw all his junk outside in the yard. I thought it would be as easy as that, but it wasn't. He came to my job while I was in the back office, rushed in, and took my keys off my desk. I was shocked – he said he was going to my house to tear up everything in it. My godfather had purchased for me a small 22 caliber pistol. Mr. Wallace became my godfather, because he said, "I can't be your sugar daddy, you cost too much. I couldn't be his mistress. I could talk to him about anything. I told him I was afraid I had made a mistake, but I was going to try to make the best of it. My godfather asked me to bring him my gun that day. He said he needed to clean it, but I later learned that after he finishes cleaning the gun, he took all the bullets out of the gun, and left one bullet in the chamber.

Christen had been calling all that day. He refused to stop harassing me. He came up with all kinds of excuses and gave reasons why I should forgive him. He promised to never put his hands on me again, and when that didn't work, he tried to threaten me. He thought he could bully me into accepting him back. I told him I was done and there was no coming back. I needed my brothers, my mama, and my sister. I needed my family. I had gotten myself into a big mess, and I had to get out of it quickly. I made a mistake, and I made it clear to him I wanted out. I ran out of the shop as I heard the front door close, and took my pistol out. I shot at him, and missed. I hit a sign in the driveway that said don't block the driveway. It hung about 5'9" on the fence. I tried to shoot again, but nothing came out of the gun. Dam, "I said", my godfather had taken the rest of the bullets out of my gun. I was angry enough to kill him; I threw the gun at him as he ran towards his car.

I worked with several guys at the used car lot. One was a very large black guy, another was a silly white guy, and two were hippies. They assured me that they weren't going to let this guy do any harm to me. Christen had taken my keys with him; I had no way to follow him. Everybody came running up front when they heard the gun go off; they asked me what had happened? I nervously explained that I had shot at Christen. I jumped in one of the used cars on the lot, and began to chase his car. Several of the guys that worked with me followed me as I chased him. We ended up at my house. I got to my house with three of the guys from my job; there stood Christen on my porch. Enraged, I begged him to come off the porch, but he just stood there like a coward. The three guys went on the porch to get him. They grabbed him, and held him down as I beat the living hell out of him with the baseball bat.

I promised the brother if he ever came close to me again, I would kill him. I went insane that day.

I didn't look at the consequences of marrying this guy while vulnerable. I didn't know enough about him before accepting his proposal. I was trying to do what the little old ladies in the Church told me to do. They told me it was a sin to have sex before getting married. The little old ladies always reminded me that if I choose to disobey I was going to hell. I didn't want to go to hell so; I married him. I thought I could trust him, because every time I saw him, he was carrying his Bible. I should have done a background search on him. The police came to my house that night, and stated they had a warrant for my arrest. I couldn't believe it. I told the police they had it wrong. The warrant couldn't be for me. This guy had taken me through hell. They said, they were arresting me for assault and shooting in the city limits. The police asked, "Lady did you shoot at the guy?" I answered, "Yes." The police asked, "Do you realize you hit that sign that read, Do Not Block the Driveway?" I did not lie - I told them, "I did." The police said the bullet went in the sign about 5'9" tall. The guy stood 5'8". One police joked, and said Ms. "You were aiming at the man's head, not his knees." I shook my head, and said uh ha. They took me to jail. I wasn't there long. I called my Godbrother, my godfather, and momma.

All of them had attorneys there to get me out, and they let me out of jail without bond, and later expunged it from my record. I had never been to jail before, and I knew I wouldn't be going back anytime soon. They didn't serve vegetables, they didn't have toothbrushes, and I couldn't take a shower when I wanted too. My attorney did a background check and learned that he had been to jail several times and had warrants out for his arrest. They went to get him and took him to jail. He stayed in jail for over a month. The short period of time he was in jail, I had peace.

When I arrived in court that morning, there were three attorneys in court waiting to defend me. I was thankful that the charges were dropped, and they released me to go home. In the short period of time that he was in jail, I hired a private investigator and learned though he married me he had proposed to another lady only weeks before I said, "I do." The ring he gave me belonged to another woman. I learned later that he used cocaine, he was abusive, and had warrants for his arrest. His mom said, when he was a child he stayed in trouble. She said, it had a lot to do with not having a relationship with his father.

He was known to use women for their money. He used the Bible to lure me in. He lied to me and told me he was a minister. He preyed on women with low self-esteem, and others that didn't have a family. Putting him in jail wasn't enough to make him leave me alone. When he got out of jail, he continued to make my life miserable. He started stalking me. I would be out having dinner or visiting with a friend, and when I look up, he would be sitting across from us or waiting for me outside. My life was a living hell. He followed me one night, and ran my car off the road. I was in front of the police station; he didn't care. He had no respect for the law. Even though I had a restraint order in place, he still came to my house, cut my telephone wires, banged on my windows, until he broke the window panes out. Thank God, I had bars on the windows, because the bars kept him from entering. My joy had been stolen.

I couldn't sleep, and I couldn't go outside without watching over my shoulders. I was being threatened every day. I wanted to run away, and hide. I married him thinking I was avoiding going to hell, but my life was a temporary hell right here on earth.

Things got so bad; I was assigned a private detective to watch over me. I made sure I had all my bases covered. I made it clear to the police department that I was living in fear. I made sure that if I had to protect my child or myself, it was documented. I was out to get him. He was going to regret ever putting his hands on me. The investigators gave me a private number to call at any time he was within 6 feet of my reach. Christen wouldn't stop calling me. He was begging me to talk with him and his pastor about getting back together. The investigators waited to catch him. I told him, he could come over, knowing I was going to set him up to go to jail. They both pulled up to my house, knocked on my door, and waited for me to let them in. The pastor came in, welcomed himself to a seat. He took out his Bible, and began reading scriptures to me from the Bible. He told me I was obligated to stay with Christen, because the Bible said, I was his wife until death departed us. I studied the Bible for myself, and read scriptures confirming that he was not my husband. I told him, I was sure that I would be forgiven for my decision to go on with my life. As they both sat in my house trying to convince me to give the marriage a chance, I asked to be excused for a moment. I told them I needed to use the restroom. I went to the restroom, and called the police. They came out quickly, and caught them both in my house. Christen and his pastor were both taken to jail that night.

It felt good to see blue lights outside my house. I felt safe, and secure. I knew the police would protect me. When the police arrived, they were loud. They had intercoms. The police told both to come out of my house with both of their hands up. Christen looked frightened; he was begging that I wouldn't have them arrested. I smiled as the police put them both in the car, but before they drove away, I ran back in the house, got the pastors Bible, and threw it in the police car. I smiled, and said you might need this. He looked at me with hate in his eyes. He had fallen into the trap.

The judge offered me a divorce, but I didn't want a divorce. I had married him based on lies, and felt the contract should be annulled, and it was. My sister said her life was a living hell also, and she was not going to tolerate an abusive relationship any longer. We both were getting free at the same time. I remembered momma saying she woke up married to Buddy, and realized that it was a mistake. She said, she wished she had gotten out of it sooner, and that the marriage kept her drinking and drugging, because she used the alcohol and drugs to sedate herself. She said, she wasn't happy. She said, she wasted a lot of her time dealing with abusive men. She said, she thought she could change the men, but she realized the longer she stayed with them, the worse she got. She said, she realized she had to change herself.

Mom had experienced so much pain that she could tell everybody what to do to avoid it. Mom wasn't around when I made the mistake of marrying this man, she was in rehab, but after I made the mistake, she said I had a choice to either stay or get out of it. I consulted counseling and asked God for forgiveness. I got me a song, and sang it until I was over that relationship. Enough was enough. He later, after several years, asked me to forgive him, I did, and then I forgot about him. My sister told me she didn't realize I had gone through the same hell she had gone through. I told her I did, however, but I didn't stay around long. He put his hands on me once, and it was over.

MOM RECOVERED

I purchased my first new home, and mom moved into my duplex after returning from rehab. The duplex was surrounded by trees, very spacious three bedrooms, two baths, sitting room, front room, front yard, and paved backyard. She was surrounded by prominent homebuyers. Craig moved back to Memphis. He said he wanted badly to continue his relationship with his child, but her grandmother just wouldn't allow it. So, he came home, and helped mom with the grandchildren. Craig moved in with Jackie for a while, and Olivodale moved in some apartments across the streets from me. Olivodale visited my sister's husband and told him that if he ever touched her again, he would kill him. That was the last time he put his hands on our sister. We were happy to have our brother's home, because we felt safe.

We were okay with living single. We were all back home now, and became the support mom needed. We talked about the good times, and shared the bad times with mom. Jackie never talked that much about the things she experienced as a child, so I talked to mom for her. I shared with a mom how her not having it together affected us. I told her about those dirty old men and what they had done. I told her how scared we were at times not knowing where she was. I told her how Jackie was left behind waiting for her to return home. I shared a lot of childhood memories with mom. Mom was now settle and no longer using drugs or alcohol, but I could see the anger in her eyes. She wanted to go back, and do something to those guys but I laugh and told mom I thought about the same thang, but God had already fixed it. They were all dead.

We did everything in our power to erase bad memories, and make her feel loved. Jackie had three girls and one son, Craig had 4 boys and 4 girls, Olivodale had 3 girls and 4 boys, and I had one son, two daughters and one god-daughter. Mom was excited to have so many grandchildren. She said, she was able to find redemption in her grandchildren. We enjoyed sitting around the dinner sharing stories with one another. It was nothing she wanted that the children or grandchildren didn't provide for her. She had 20 years of hard times, and certainly deserved all the love we had to give to her. Mom got stronger, and recovery had begun.

We were all happy to see her improve. Mom was smiling again, and all the children, and grandchildren contributed to her happiness. Her skin was peachy yellow again, with that wavy short haircut, and she was happy.

Our family celebrated Christmas with plenty of gifts. The children all gathered at mom's house. They would go to bed anxious for the next day to come so they could rise early and open their gifts. We would slowly come in on Christmas day. I would be the first to get there. Mom would be in the kitchen cooking and playing that good old blues. As mom cooked, I watched her, memories of the hard and bad times came back, and tears gathered in my eyes. This time it wasn't tears of sadness, it was because mom was back. She was happy again.

Mom accepted the things she could not change, and began to work on the things she could change. She attempted to build a relationship with her mother and her sister.

We all trust mom with our deepest secrets, and we trust what she had to say. Mom didn't agree with wrong doing, because she had done enough for all of us. She could identify predators with bad behaviors. Mom taught us all not to do the things she had done to hurt herself. I never lied to my mother, because she had experienced so much street life - there was nothing I couldn't openly share with her that she could not tell me how to handle. She reminded us that we didn't need an abusive, alcoholic or drug driven relationship. She taught us to respect ourselves, and to have morals, and set standards for our lives. She told me to trust the spirit, and she often reminded me that it was a force, the spirit of God that taught her right from wrong.

She told her boys never to put their hands on a woman or abuse them verbally, and always to take care of their children. She taught us to be independent of others, and to accomplish those things our hearts desired. Mom always said use people if they had something to use; and if they didn't have anything to use, don't use them. Dad taught us not to abuse people even if they had something to use. Dad and mom remain friends through all their hardships. We were blessed that they remain, friends, because we needed both.

After 22 long years of repeating drug, and abusive driven relationships, she admitted that the only man she ever loved was her husband, the father of her children, our dad. Our father was a man that set examples of what a good husband, father, and man was. I grew up knowing how to choose good men. I could measure them by my father behaviors and mannerisms.

I knew I had some strongholds to break, because I made the mistake of marrying for five days, because of what I thought Mr. Perfect was. I learned the hard way that Mr. Perfect had a very little to do with what a man looks like from the outside but more of what he looks like in the inside. I found out that Mr. Perfect wasn't because of what a person had, but because of the unconditional love. There was so much I learned about choosing a spouse. The little old ladies meant well. However, I learn that if we are not careful choosing our spouse or companion, we may go to hell right here on earth.

STEPMOTHER WAS NICE

Our new stepmother was the glue that helped us stick to our mom and dad. There were numerous times the orphanage home could have taken us. However, regardless of what mom was going through our stepmother helped dad raise us and when we wanted to see our mom, she encouraged us to do so. She never said one bad word about our mother, and for that I love her. She wasn't that bad person we thought she was after all. I remembered all of us outside in Chicago running under the firer hydrates. She was out playing and running with us. After all, she was only 25 years old. We were in dad's convertible mustang. We were all in the car with the convertible top down, and she was speeding through the water. The police pulled her over to the side for speeding. We all went to jail. They called the paddy wagon, and we all were taken to jail. Dad had to come for us. Stepmother was like a big child herself. I realized she was looking for the same thing we were looking for, and that was love. We learned she wasn't selfish, unlike dad's other woman. She didn't try to take dad away from us. She spent time with the grandchildren in Chicago, and helped the boys as much as she could. The boys stayed with dad, Jackie, and I stayed with mom. Mom was closer to the girl's children, because they were all in the same city. Our stepmother never tried taking the place of our mom.

She became our friend. Olivodale said, he wished she was his girlfriend, he like her big chocolate legs.

Craig didn't say much, but he didn't have anything bad to say. Jackie had a hard time getting along with any of mom's or dad's companions. She had been abused, and accused many times, and she didn't trust any of them. It was great to see my mother, and stepmother have a friendship. Mom appreciated her for taking care of us, and I did too.

I was happy. I remembered dad brushing my hair, it didn't look the best, but it worked. When Margaret came into dad's life he didn't have to worry about combing my hair; things got better for us all. We were a family with structure.

Mom was smiling once again, and her beautiful personality was once again drawing people to her. One would have never known mom had been through so much danger and lived such a dysfunctional life. If one judged her by her outer appearance, it would be hard to tell how much pain mom had experienced and how much pain, she carried around daily from not having her parents in her life. I often told mom she had done everything but died. She had a gift to discern what was good, and bad for us, and she often talked to us about the consequences of bad choices. She applauded those things that were good, and reprimanded us about those things that were bad for us. She wasn't ashamed of her life or her mistakes; she shared her testimonies with others that had fallen into similar traps she had to get out of.

THE GIFT OF PROPHECY

Her children, grandchildren, and others relied upon her gift of prophecy and her discerning spirit. While I was in New York studying my acting career, there would be many people stopping by to pick up flowers, but some stopped by just to have an encouraging talk with mom. Mom shared her life stories to help others heal and stop cycles of domestic violence, abusing drugs and alcohol with many. We were all happy that mom had recovered from abusing alcohol and drugs. I could depend on her encouraging me when I was discouraged. She was able to inspire, motivate and help me make good decisions. I knew I had to stick to bringing my dream of becoming an actress to reality because mom said it would be another way for me to help people. I asked her why she felt acting would help others; she told me that I would have many stories I could share. She said you could start by telling mine.

I GOT THE RIGHT
ONE BABY

After getting over a broken heart and running into that one bad relationship my girlfriend and I went out to a club Downtown Memphis. We were out enjoying the music and dancing. I spotted this handsome guy sitting on the other side of the club. He was quiet and quite attractive. The host of the party asked all guys that had on jeans to enter a best dressed competition. He was sharp. He had on a long jean jacket, with jean pants and leather boots. Several ladies, and I insisted that he enter the competition. He was bashful, and wouldn't enter. The crowd began clapping and cheering him on. The crowd didn't give him a choice, so he walked on the stage, and the women began to scream. I screamed so loud I lost my voice. The competition paid $100.00, and he won. He went over got the money and headed toward the men's room. I premeditated a plan to get to know him. I watched his every move. Once he went into the men's room, I went and stood by the door. I waited for him to come out the restroom and put my foot out to trip him. He stumbled. I said excuse me and immediately started a conversation with him about his outfit. I told him how handsome he was. He said thanks and began to walk off. I said, "Excuse me, I'm not done". He said, "Oh I apologize". I told him that I had lost my voice. He apologized and asked if there was anything he could do to help me. I said yes, I need some lemons. He asked, "Where can I get lemons." I said at the grocery store. He said, "Ok". I got in my car, he got in his, and we drove towards the store. Once we got to the store, we went in and got the lemons. He said now what I told him he would have to come to my house, roll the lemons and I would suck them. He laughed and agreed. He followed me to my house. My son was visiting my mother for the weekend. We went in the house; he rolled the lemons on the kitchen floor. I sucked one for my sore throat. I then asked him if he knew how to play jacks. He said he did. I was shocked that he answered yes, because most guys would have said something stupid, like I'm a man. Oh well. So, I told him I wanted to play a game. I wanted to play jacks and whoever won could make a request. He went along with the game. I won, and when I did, I asked him to give me a kiss. He kissed me lightly.

That was the beginning to us dating. We dated for three years, and we got pregnant with our first daughter, and shortly thereafter our second daughter was born. I carefully picked him, because he was a part of me stopping generational curses and dysfunctional cycles from repeating in my life. I remembered the vow I made to myself not to ever get into another domestic violent relationship. I choose him based on the type of man my father was. He had a lot of characteristics like my father. He was spiritual, handsome, a provider, honest, a good father, didn't fight, did not use drugs, and he wasn't controlling, arrogant or jealous. He was an introverted person, and very laid back. I shared my life experiences with him, and he shared his with me. He had a very loving mother and a stepfather that supported him. He told me he never got to know his father, but the man that he did know was his dad. He talked about his big momma and how much he loved her. He told me the stories of cooking for her and living with her until she died.

THE ROADMAP TO A FUNCTIONING LIFESTYLE

Both of my parents had ways that transferred to me. I was raised in both a dysfunctional environment, and functional environment. Both lifestyles taught me how to deal with different kind of people in all walks of life. I learn street sense from mom and common sense from dad. I broke another cycle by continuing my education so that I could make intelligent decisions and break the curse of living in poverty. I used the experience of growing up in a dysfunctional environment surrounded by poverty, to help me identify those that needed help. I was able to write this book to those that were stuck in poverty and to those that had been abused intentionally and unintentionally. It was my prayer that someone would read something in the story that would help them to change, break re-occurring curses and pull-down strongholds. It was my hope that the story would do just as mom said and that is help to heal the land. I knew how to deal with thugs, ghetto, alcoholics, and homeless people.

I used the experience of living around wealth in a functional civilized environment to choose the lifestyle I wanted for myself and family. I knew how to deal with wealthy, educated, business and professional people, because I pursued education, traveled the world and met people from all walks of life. It was diversity that helped me to understand that I could recreate myself. As an adult, I realized I had to break habits that I picked up from others. I had work to do. However, recreating myself was worth the work. I made a vow that all the bad things mom experienced I would use to break the cycles of generational curses. I learned from my mother's mistakes and poor choices not to repeat the cycle; I knew if it didn't work for her it certainly wouldn't work for me. Her life became a road map that led me to live a better lifestyle, unlike the one she lived.

I used the roadmap to make good decisions. Once I identified the issues and dysfunctional behavioral that had hurt my family, I knew what not to do and what habits I had to break. Some were easy while others were not. I knew that drinking to sedate my fears, disappointments and hardships wouldn't be an outlet or solution to finding a better way of life. So, I stopped drinking. I had friends and associates that asked why? I never said it was wrong to have a sociable drink, but for me, I wasn't taught to socialize with alcohol. I was taught to sedate my fears, my pain, my voids and my hardships with alcohol so for me drinking wasn't an option. I learn that marrying for money or selfish reasons wouldn't fill the void that existed in me. One of my voids was to become what I was created to be. I began to fulfill voids as I faced my truth. From that, I learned that only I could fulfill the purpose God had for me. Money from others was only a quick fix. However, my journey to success came when I was able to share life experiences with others to help them find their way from poverty to wealth. I knew that tolerating physical abuse or verbal abuse wasn't worth the misery of living in a chaotic environment, but I also learned from mom that I too had to control what came out of my mouth and to keep my hands to myself. I vowed not to belittle myself by using my body to gain material wealth. I was thankful that God forgave me, and that prayer worked because money certainly couldn't cure diseases or the feeling of guilt. It was clear that stealing from others wouldn't satisfy my lust for success there was nothing another person had that I wanted so badly that I would take it. I learned that a closed mouth wouldn't get fed. I learn to ask for what I wanted, and if one showed me favor, I was thankful however if not I worked for those material things I wanted from life. Some came sooner than others and some required planning and setting goals. It was clear that unless I uncovered the truth and lies to my children, they wouldn't know how to avoid the generational curses that had travel on to me. The truth is known to hurt, however during my journey of learning the truth it felt good to discover that there were rumors and lies, misinformed information and unintentional things that occurred. However, once I uncovered those things and learned to discuss and communicate with others openly, I healed. It was then that I was able to forgive and share those stories with my children. The precious part of uncovering the hidden deadly secrets was this time I didn't bury the pain; I got rid of the pain. Did I forget any of it? No, but I used it as a tool to choose the life I fantasized. I knew that keeping deadly secrets wouldn't stop the cycle from reoccurring and by hiding the truth of those bad decisions I made wouldn't make me any greater. What made me greater is when I accepted that we all fall short, but we can get back up again. We can make better decisions about our lives. However, it was a fact that by avoiding all the things that hurt my mother and by working hard not to carry the cycle would stop the dysfunctional curses from traveling through me to my children and others. Mom's roadmap gave me a reason to be excited about recreating myself so that I could share the truth the whole truth and nothing but the truth with others. Dad lifestyle taught me that it was up to me to earn the lifestyle I wanted to live. He taught me that other's wealth wouldn't validate who I was.

While great-grandmother taught me that prayer only works if I believe, have faith and trust that I could recreate myself and heal. We all had a choice of whether we were going to carry the dysfunctional cycles that we grew up around as children or whether we were going to stop the cycle by breaking the generational curses that were transferred to us and live a lifestyle that was functional. Becoming a curse breaker was work, and I had lots of it to do. I was the youngest child of four, and my siblings did all they could to protect me. Yet there were still those predators that ruthlessly took advantage of us. I could have easily been angry with mom for some of the things that happened to me as a child, but it was easier and healthier to love her, forgive and understand that mom had a sickness. I was happy to have the courage to face the truth and work through it so that I could help my family and others to heal.

I learned from dating guys that they all had issues, but it was what issues I was willing to deal with. After two daughters Dallas and I separated, I wanted to be sure we were marrying for love, and not for only the children sake. The children were indeed important, but I was making sure I wasn't falling into a trap that mom had once fallen into. I wanted to break the curse of single parenting, but I also wanted to find love and be loved. During our separation, we continued to provide for our daughters and son. We agreed to take the time apart to make sure we were marrying for love.

FORGIVING

Jackie purchased mom a house. Oliviodale moved next door to her. It was a nice small two-bedroom house, enough room for her and the grandchildren whenever they wanted to visit. The grandchildren always visit mom and frequently stayed overnight with her. Mom's grandchildren could do no wrong. We all said she got it right with them, because she had made so many mistakes with us.

We were a close family. My siblings and I pitched in to make sure all the children had what they needed. My son said it made him angry that he had to share me with his cousins. He didn't understand the theory of the old cliché, that it takes a village to raise children and that is what our family became during the hardships of my parent's lives. We became the village to help one another explain, express, guide and direct our families out of a dysfunctional lifestyle. After all, mom made it clear that whatever we were going through to stick together.

We were happy to see that mom was happy. Once again that peachy color skin was glowing. Her pretty hair was flowing, and that bright smile was back. She was celebrating 20 years of sobriety. Sunday was once again family day. She enjoyed cooking for us, and we enjoyed eating her food. Jackie was back living in California. Olivodale was living next door; I was in New York studying, Acting and Craig was married and helping mom as needed. There wasn't much mom needed that the grandchildren or her children didn't provide. She felt loved. Dad often visit and brought our stepmother. It was beautiful to see two women work together for the sake of the family.

Jackie brought money to support mom, and to provide for her children when they were with her. I remembered Jackie leaving $3,000.00 with mom in case of an emergency. Mom used some of it gambling at the casino. Mom said the children had stolen some of it. Mom admitted that her going to the casino was getting out of control. Soon gambling became a habit that caused problems for mom, and the house was facing foreclosure.

SHARING AND CARING

Mom said she wanted to move. We were concerned but convinced that the move would make her happy. We packed her clothes and moved her. One thing that we all knew that made mom happy was the grandchildren. They often spent time at mom's house. We were concerned that the apartments she was moving into had rules that the tenants weren't allowed overnight quest. I was concern that mom was going back into an environment that could lead her back to where she had overcome. Though the place overlooked the city skyline a lot of the people there were sick. Some of them were depressed and other suffered from mental illnesses. But like before mom became a mentor to those people that were sick, and others that were using drugs. She inspired them with her stories of once being addicted to drugs and alcohol. She shared many stories of domestic violence, verbal abuse, and mental abuse. She was able to motivate and encourage others to get help.

Mom said she enjoyed sharing her stories with others. She said, though she was giving apart of herself she was also receiving something by giving. She felt that by sharing her truth, she was releasing that pain she once had buried. Mom received a fixed income, and though we provided her with her needs, She said she had wants and took a job taking care of elderly people twice a week. She started with an elderly man. The little elderly-man made mom smile. She said, he reminded her of a father she never got to know. She said, she learned to love him. She told me stories of how she cooked for him, took him out to walk in the mornings and sat on the porch and had coffee with him. She said, he filled a void in her life. She told me how she thought she was going there to give something to him, but instead, she got something. She talked about how he told her she reminded him of his daughter that had been killed in a car accident. They were good for one another; I could tell because mom would often say I'm going in to take care of dad today. One-night mom called me and told me he was sick, and she was afraid that he wasn't going to make it. I could hear the fear in her voice. I was sad, because I knew mom had fallen in love with the little old man and losing something she loved wasn't going to be good for her. He died. Mom smile didn't look the same for weeks.

Shortly after he died, she began caring for a retired school teacher. The lady had been in a car accident. The neighbors said bad things about her. One neighbor told mom she dated the married ladies husband down the street and, she had a reputation for being a home breaker. She was bedridden and couldn't do anything for herself. Mom had to feed, bathe and listen to her groan. She said, there was a very uncomfortable spirit in the house. She said, the lady was mean, and she started resenting her. She often complained about going to work and began complaining of headaches. One day she came home, and one of the guys offered her a downer to relax. She took the depressant and found herself occasionally using them to suppress her depression. She didn't like her job, but she kept going, because she said she needed the money.

We told mom we could take care of her needs, and that she didn't have to continue working for the lady if it was bothering her, but she insisted that she was okay and wanted to keep working. On several occasions, I called mom, and notice that her speech was slurred. I was concerned that mom might have been excessively using pain pills. She got a bit angry when I asked her, so I backed off.

Mom had given up on having relationships with men, because she said those days for fighting were over. She said she wasn't going to let her hate for men make her deal with another woman. She withdrew herself from relationships completely. Mom always told me never to allow a man to put his hands on me. She made it clear that if a man hit me once he would do it again. We talked about the verbal abuse, and how if a man degraded me or spoke in a mean way to cut the relationship off. Mom said, if a man talks bad to a woman, fighting would soon follow. She said verbal and physical abuse goes hand in hand. She reminded me of the type of man our father was and told me dad was a good man and had the qualities I should look for in a man. She described dad as a responsible man that provided for his family and took care of his children. She went on to say that daddy was a Godly man and he was humble, but strong. She said, she created the problem that caused them to divorce.

DEATH WAITS
FOR NO ONE

Grandmother became ill with cancer. My mother said, she had accepted the things she couldn't change with her mom, and was working on those things she could to better their relationship they had begun working on their relationship, and shared some of the stories they both needed to talk about, but they didn't get a chance to finish. Mom said, that grandmother told her about the abusive relationships she had gotten herself in with her husband, James. Then grandmother said, she wanted to come back for them, but her husband didn't want any more kids. James had three kids of his own. Mom said she told her mother how bad it hurt all of them when she left. She told her for a long time she blamed her for the many mistakes she made in her life, because she didn't have her to help guide her path. Mom said, she was happy to hear her mother say that she loved her, but she was sad that she had to wait until she was dying to hear it. I told mom, "Mom grandmother probably told you she loved you many times, but because, you were drinking you didn't remember." She agreed. The next day grandmother died. Mom got worse. I could see the pain in her eyes, and I could hear it in her voice. I was afraid for mom and worried that she was relapsing. All I could do is pray.

Mom loved her brother – he was a great man. He was educated and had spent time in the military.

There were rumors that the military caused him to have mental issues. I recalled him telling me how he would see people get shot that was standing right next to him. He shared horror stories about little babies, and elderly people getting killed. He was married to a classy woman. I always said I wanted to be just like his wife when I grew up because she kept her hair in order, dressed well and spoke intelligently. They had one son. We all loved our Uncle Percy. He never talked much, but when he came to visit, we knew we were going to have fun. As time passed, Uncle Percy started drinking and using drugs. He and auntie divorced. He wanted to be with his mother. I recall mom saying he moved to St. Louis for a while, but things didn't work out, so he moved back to Mississippi. He lived in a little house in the country. There were no lights. It was difficult to see him like that, because I remembered him to be that uncle that came to Mississippi to buy us a hamburger, ice cream, and cookies. I remembered him teaching me how to drive his convertible corvette. He too blamed his mental illness for not getting to know his father, and never spending the quality time needed with his mother. Mom and her brother were close, they communicated well with one another. He was diagnosed with cancer. My aunt went to get him and brought him to Memphis. I was at his bedside when he took his last breath and died. His death left mom and her sister sad.

Mom was near celebrating 21 years of sobriety. Years ago, mom had been diagnosed with diabetes and liver problems; it came from the years of abusing alcohol and both street and over the counter drugs. The doctor told her if she ever started using either again it would cause a serious setback. The doctor told her, because she wasn't using drugs, and alcohol her health had improved significantly; however, he reminded her that the use of nicotine, and the abuse of pain pills would only cause her health to be impacted negatively.

Depression had taken over. Mom was sleeping a lot. I felt taking a trip may help her, so we packed our bags and headed to California to see her friend Jay, Jay. We were both excited to see that Jay, Jay was doing great she was no longer drinking or using drugs. She was now counseling people that had fallen slave to drugs and alcohol. I told Jay-Jay I was concerned that mom was using pain pills again and I was worried. Mom had taken a nap. Jay-Jay and I went through her luggage and found codeine. I cried. I asked her about the pills when she awaken. She told me I was invading on her privacy. I apologize to her and shared with her my concerns of seeing her backslide to the addiction she had struggled to overcome almost twenty-one years ago. She insisted that the doctor had given them to her for depression.

I didn't press the issue any further. Instead, I went into the kitchen fixed us a sandwich and watched a movie.

I was concern that mom's environment wasn't healthy for her. I insisted she move, but she insisted she was doing great. I was invited to bid on a house at the courthouse Downtown Memphis that had gone into foreclosure. I was desperate to find mom a better environment to live. I was running late because I had gotten stuck in traffic. I prayed, and prayed that I wouldn't miss the opportunity because it was the perfect place for mom. When I arrived no one was there, but the attorneys. They were closing the auction, but when they realized I was there to bid, they allowed me. I was the only person biding. The attorneys accepted my bid. My siblings agreed to help me pay for it. We wanted to make her transition easy.

SURPRISE

I was excited and happy to surprise her. I called her and told her I had something to show her. I told her I would pick her up within the hour. When I arrived, she was sitting out front like usual talking to neighbors. I loved her bright colors, she looked pretty, as she approached the car she smiled, and asked where are we going? I said, "Not shopping." I laughed. She laughed and said, "Well there's no need for me to get in the car." We continued to laugh as she opened the door. We drove and drove and drove, and talked and talked and talked. I asked mom again if she wanted to move from the high rises. She said, not really, but if it were on a lake or surrounded by water, she would. We pulled up to the house, and I gave her the keys. She asked, "What are these for?" I said this house is yours. She looked shocked, but not too excited. She opened the door looked around and said I don't think I want to live here. I asked, why? She said, "Someone was murdered in this house." I said, "Mom no one was murdered in this house." She insisted a woman was murdered in the house. I put the house up for rent.

DENIAL

Mom continued to deny self-medicating herself with pain pills until one night my sister found her in her apartment in a diabetic coma. I was off in Wilmington North Carolina filming in a movie. My sister called me, and told me I needed to rush home. We were all scared, I caught a flight, and got to the hospital. Things didn't look good. The doctor said, she had overdosed on pain pills. We called our father, and he said pray her through it, and stick together. He said, he was on his way. Her children, grandchildren, sister, nieces, nephews, and friends all came together in prayer. I remembered my sister turning the lights out in the room, and said let's pray for mom's forgiveness, and her soul to be delivered. I turned the lights back on because I wasn't ready for mom to die. I felt she was not prepared to go.

Oliviodale left the hospital and went to the Mississippi River. Mom always told us that we could find answers, and peace at the water. We believed in the signs of water. I also believed like mom that ladybugs were a sign of good things. I trust what my mother taught me because she had experienced the good and the bad in her life. I grew up believing that those things that hurt mom would hurt me and, I believed that the signs mom used to help her make it through hard times would also help me. My brother said he was going to take a walk on the river that night. He said, he was searching for answers, hoping that mom was going to be okay. He said, he knew mom had taken pills that night, because he went with her to purchase them. Oliviodale said, he felt guilty. He said, he should not have taken mom to get the drugs. He said, he felt responsible. He told the doctors to look for codeine in her system. The doctors listen to him and found an excessive amount of codeine in her system. They immediately started detoxing her. Oliviodale admitted he didn't go to the river to take a walk; he went to the Mississippi River to commit suicide. He told us the only reason he didn't commit suicide that night was that he believes in the signs of the water. He said mom had told him if the river was flowing down that was a bad sign, but if the river was flowing upward, it was a good sign. Olivodale said, "The River was flowing upward, so he didn't commit suicide." Oliviodale said, "I ran back to the hospital, and I yelled mom is going to be all right." He screamed, "The water is flowing upwards." Mom started making improvements the next day. We all continued to pray. Mom had been in a coma for 10 days, but we prayed, kept the faith and she recovered. I could hear my great-grandmother voice in my head saying prayer works if you have faith. Regardless of how mean she was, she taught us about God.

The next day we met with our dad and went to see mom. The doctors told us they had good news.

They told us mom was awake. We all ran in the room excited! Mom acted as she had never been in the coma. The first thing from mom's mouth was, "Where is my money?" My oldest brother Craig assured her that he had her money and her purse in a safe place. Craig always watched out for mom. When we were young and got misplaced, Craig never left mom's side. He went wherever she went. Now that he was an adult he took mom wherever she needed to go. He took her on road trips, fishing and to her ceramic classes. Mom was released from the hospital early that next morning. We were all happy to have mom back.

THE DREAM OF ACTING

I continued classes in New York and gave my floral business the quality time needed for it to grow. It was always a desire that laid dormant in my heart to be an actress. I continued to travel different cities to explore acting opportunities. It was hard finding the agent needed to get the break I was searching for and sometimes I found myself wanting to give up. However honestly, I didn't know what I was searching for. I just knew that I wanted to feel fulfilled. I wanted to know my purpose. Mom encouraged me to go; she told me that she would keep the shop and help with my children. She was always supportive of those things I desired. She told me she wanted to make sure she gave me the support she never got from her mother.

In 1997 a film maker by the name of George Tillman gave my headshots to a Memphis Casting Director for a motion picture being filmed in the area. The movie was called "A Family Thang." The leading characters were Robert Duvall and James Earl, Jones. I received a call to audition for a small part. I went in to meet the casting director and received the part of a businesswoman. I had no speaking lines, but I was grateful for my part. I worked next to the lead actors.

Regardless of what mom was going through she encouraged and motivated us to pursue those things that were good, and she told us to avoid the traps that others could easily set for us. She not only supported us, but she helped us to make major decisions in our lives. I was thankful that mom helped me with my first boy child and my girls because, I needed her. She knew how it felt to be a teenage parent because, she too had gotten pregnant at the young age of 16. She did all she could to help me with my 1st baby boy, and I was able to continue my education as an accountant. I learned to appreciate my mom's struggles. I could share with her my deepest secrets. She guided me when I made mistakes, and she celebrated me when I accomplished my goals. She was my mother, and she was my friend. I was able to consult with her about every major decision I made. When I told her how excited I was about going into acting, she told me to go for it, and I did.

ARE YOU, MY DAD

Oliviodale continued soul searching to find his identity. He wanted to know if the rumors of him belonging to another man were true. He went to Sears one day to meet and introduce himself to this supposed to be a father, Mr. Harry. He went into the store and asked one of the men if Mr. Harry was there. The man pointed Mr. Harry out. Olivodale said, they had one thing in common, and that was they both were mechanics. He walked up to him, said hello and started a conversation by asking him a few questions. He asked, "Do you know Ethan Cole? Mr. Harry answered, "Yes I do." He asked, "Do you know Oliviodale Cole? Mr. Harry answered, "Yes." He then said, "I'm Oliviodale". Mr. Harry then asked, "Where have you been boy?" Oliviodale told him, he had been in Chicago. Mr. Harry stood there starring at Olivodale. Oliviodale asked, "Are you, my dad?" He replied, "That's what your mom said." The conversation continued as Oliviodale shared some information with him about himself and his 5,000 square feet mechanic shop. Oliviodale had been doing well with his shop until some of his staff started stealing money from him. His staff had written bad checks, and they left him in a financial bind. He told Mr. Harry, he was at risk of losing the business after owning it for 8 years. Mr. Harry said, he was sorry to hear and offered no financial support.

Oliviodale left Sears that evening disappointed. He said, he was disappointed, because the man didn't act excited about meeting him. He said, he wondered how could a man have a son age 33-years-old and never reach out to him. Oliviodale was hurt. He said, he felt he had abandoned him. Oliviodale gave up his business. Oliviodale went to dad and asked him why he never said anything about this man? Dad replied, "Oliviodale I never listened to your mom because she knew how to get what she wanted." Dad said, she had her ways, and he never thought it was true. He said to him, he was born a Cole and that's all that mattered. Oliviodale not knowing what to say, walked away. He was left to deal with the pain. When he confronted mom she told him, she was young and, she had made a mistake - she said she didn't know if it was true or not. She asked him to forgive her for being young and foolish.

When my brother told me what he had done I told him, I didn't need him, I never desired him, nor did I ever miss him, in fact, our father was the only man we knew as dad. My father had taught me what was right from wrong and there was nothing this man could offer me. I had overcome many hardships, and I was now an adult. The hard part was over. All I needed from him was the truth so that I could continue writing the story. My sister convinced us that the man was wealthy, she talked about his entrepreneurial skills. A light bulb went off in my head. I started thinking like my momma; maybe he can give us some money.

As I pondered over the possibilities I called my aunt and, I asked her to tell me what she knew about it. She told me the rumor of me being his daughter wasn't true. Auntie said, I wasn't his daughter, she never admitted Olivodale was his son, but she did confirm that mom had an affair with him around the time that he was conceived. Auntie suggested that I called his brother and talked to him.

Uncle Hatley, is what I called his brother, but I didn't call him Uncle Hatley because he was my father's brother. I called him Uncle Hatley, because he was my aunt's ex-husband. When I thought about that, I realized that my mother and her sister both were messing around with brothers. The only person really knew if the rumor was true would have been our mother or Mr. Harry, and there was a great possibility that they didn't know the truth.

I wondered if the rumors ever bothered Mr. Harry enough to want to know the truth about the possibility of being my brother's dad or was he okay with taking the rumor to his grave with him. I found that many people in my family and other families, had buried many childhoods, adolescent and adult dysfunctional behavior and memories in the bottles of alcohol and some had suppressed and sedated their pain with drugs. I'm sure some of mom's drinking alcohol and using drugs was to sedate the rumors and lies that she never cared to discuss, while some of the sedating were to deal and tolerate the abuse and domestic relationships that left her empty and unhappy. Seemly once mom stopped sedating herself with the drugs and alcohol she was more open to discuss her truth.

Dad too had buried a few rumors inside, but the rumor of paternity issues didn't appear to bother our father, because he loved and provided for all of us the same. However, the lies and rumors bothered my brother differently. He choose to hold on to the pain and used alcohol to sedate himself. I couldn't understand how this stranger could cause so much pain for him. I called his brother, Uncle Hatley, he told me he knew my mother and his brother had an affair, but he verified that his brother wasn't messing around with mom when she conceived me. I gave Uncle Hatley, my number and asked him to tell his brother to please call me. I waited for his call.

The next day Margaret and Dad came to Memphis. We were going to Biloxi to enjoy the water and relax. I wasn't sure what time they were arriving. However, I didn't want them to be present if Mr. Harry called because I didn't want to insult my father by talking to a stranger about our pass. However, as soon as dad and Margaret walked in the door, Mr. Harry called. I greeted dad and Margaret with a hug and told them to excuse me for a moment.

I went to the back to make sure dad didn't hear me talking. Mr. Harry introduced himself and went on to say his brother had told him I wanted to talk with him. I told him I would have to call him back, because my dad and stepmother had walked in and we were on our way out of town. I asked for his number and promised to give him a call later in the week. My dad, Martha and I got in my truck and went off to the waters. We had a great time. The water was flowing upwards.

The following week I told my brother, Mr. Harry had called me. He asked me what he had to say. I told him nothing, because I didn't give him time. I told my brother maybe we should check him out. I was thinking like my mother; maybe he does have money. My brother and I laughed as we talked about making a deal with him on the back-pay child support he hadn't paid. We laughed our butts off, because we were in our thirties talking about collecting back pay for child support. Oliviodale said, if he didn't have money, he would take his toolbox. I suggested before talking to him we get his address from the operator and drive by his house to see where he lived. We were acting like mom and her brother. They often got themselves a drink and did some daring things together. I told my brother the last time I had gotten drunk was on the Mississippi River with mom. We continued to laugh. My brother had me cracking up. He said, "one more time won't hurt you." I said okay, I passed him my cup and told him to pour up. The more we drank, the more my personality was changing. I was ready to approach this man. We both were getting loud.

We looked up his address and learned his house was near mom's old neighborhood. The closer we got to his address the surer, I felt he didn't have money. We pulled up to his address, and there was overgrown grass standing almost 4ft. tall in his yard. I told my brother, I wanted to get the hell away from there, because it looked like he needed us to cut his yard. It was funny because we were sneaking trying to see if he had those luxury cars my sister had told us about. We slowly drove to the back of his house, and all I saw was an old Chevrolet car, it was covered with bird mess on it. I looked over at Oliviodale as he continued to self-medicate himself and we both agreed things weren't looking to prosperous. My brother didn't want to face the truth that the man likely was broke and needed us more than we needed him. Olivodale said, let's knock on the door. I said, "No not tonight." I almost hit a pole trying to get away from the man's house. His yard was a mess. The house was old and raggedy.

All I could see was a man that needed us because we certainly didn't have a need for him. We laugh all the way home. I dropped my brother off at his house and went home. I was so happy that man wasn't my father. The next day I felt horrible from drinking and knew why I no longer would sedate myself.

I waited a couple of weeks and decided to call Mr. Harry. Mr. Harry answered the telephone with a pleasant hello. I said, hello and then proceeded to ask him a few questions. I asked him to tell me the truth about the rumors of him being my brother's father. He said the same thing my aunt and uncle told me. I ask him, "How does it feel not to know the truth?" I said, Mr. Harry, "Did you ever care?" He said that he never came forth as Oliviodale's father because our father was a good man and a hardworking man that provided for his family. He said, he knew he was a good man, but my momma was a pretty woman, with a beautiful smile that lured him in with her beauty. He went on to say; he regretted he crossed the line, because he never wanted to be thought of as a home breaker. I got quiet. He said, "Are you still there?" I answered, "Yes sir," He said, I'm sorry I never thought about the outcome of my actions. I couldn't say much because, I realized that a lot of us don't think about the outcome of our actions. I certainly had done things in my life that had I thought about the consequences or the outcome perhaps I would have not done them. I told him thanks for communicating with me, and before I hung up the telephone, I said Mr. Harry, I really appreciate and love my dad. Everything went silent. I asked are you still there? He said yes. I said bye and hung up the telephone. It wasn't easy facing the truth, but the more I did, the more I found that the truth was healing me. It was my wish for my siblings to heal also, but I soon realize everyone had to make their own decisions. My heart ached as I witnessed the cycle continue to some, but my heart rejoiced as I watched the cycle be broken with others.

UNCOVER THE
UGLY MEMORIES

There were many ugly childhood memories that needed to be uncovered so that the beautiful moments we shared during mom's hardships could be remembered. As I continued to search and face my family truth, I was able to identify the dysfunctional behavioral that were transferred on to me. In doing so, I discovered lies and rumors that had circulated throughout the family for years. The rumors and lies that stayed swept under the rugs for years had caused some to be confused, while others were left feeling rejected, unloved and unwanted.

Although, the elderly church mothers, great-grandmother, and mom meant well they all shared misinformed information, because they too didn't have the proper guidance needed to live a functional lifestyle. It was clear that they were dealing with curses that had been transferred on to them. They shared what they were taught. I'm certain none of them intended to hurt us with the information they shared.

When my sister and I took that ride down memory lane, there was no returning back until I uncovered all the layers. Once the layers got uncovered, I discovered how to heal. My healing began when I identified all the dysfunctional behavior that had transferred on to me and began working on getting rid of each stronghold, one at a time. I then found that to go from rags to riches I had work to do, I had to recreate myself. The first thing I had to do is face and accept the truth, the next thing I began to do was stop doing those things that hurt my mother, father, and ancestors, then I had to undo those things that I had been taught that had me living in a fantasy world, the next thing I had to do was become a curse breaker and stop dysfunctional cycles. Last, I had to expose lies, break bad habits and honestly communicate my discovery of truth to prevent the bad behaviors from continuing and traveling through me to my children and others.

I was so grateful to have learned the truth. I thought to myself what if I couldn't call mom when I needed someone to share my fears with? I went on and on and on. I cried out to God, because I was grateful to have a mother that shared the truth the whole truth and nothing but the truth with me. I rushed to call her to tell her the good news. I thought about mom laying in the hospital bed in that coma. I dropped to my knees and gave God thanks that he didn't take my mother.

My siblings and I dealt with our pain differently. I death with my pain through recreating myself and becoming a writer. While some of us repeated the cycle of her bad habits, experiences, and behaviors. Researching our family history wasn't easy, it was hard, shocking and painful. There were many ugly memories, rumors and hardships momma went through. We lived a chaotic life at times, because we went through those things with her. There were layers of dysfunctional behavior that had been swept under the rugs. No one wanted to talk about those ugly childhood memories, but everybody was whispering and keeping secrets about the damage that the sexual abuse, teenage pregnancy, domestic violence, drugs, alcohol, and poverty had done. I wanted to talk about it because I wanted it to stop.

It was obvious that single parenting, teenage pregnancy, domestic violence, drug addiction, alcohol, sexual abuse, scandals, custody issues and paternity issues were constantly traveling from one generation to another. It was clear that cycles were repeating themselves.

As I continued to research my mother and father's lives, I learned that a lot of my good decisions came from my mother's bad decisions. I felt bad that our mother had to experience so many devastating things, but I learned to appreciate her for the knowledge I gathered from her bad experiences. When I was younger, I thought that mom was showing us how to live our lives, but after getting older, I knew that she was teaching me how not to live my life.

Reflecting on all the raggedy shotgun houses, we grew up in gave me more reasons to appreciate my two, three and four-story homes and mansions.

Our mother's story became the book that helped me to begin breaking generational curses and pulling down demonic strongholds in my family.

I had no room for jealousy, bitterness, anger, hate, envy, competitiveness, boastful spirits or arrogance in my life. I knew these things would cause one to eventually use a substance that could lead them down a road to no return. I asked for forgiveness of my children for any unknown pain my bad decisions possibly could have caused and prayed that they accepted and took upon the challenge to also become a curse breaker by identifying dysfunctional behavior and stopping it from traveling through them to the next generation to come.

I accepted the things I could not change growing up as children and began to work on those things I could change. I learned to trust the very thing great-grandmother stressed to heal our family, which was God and prayer. I learned to pray for my family to stop the generational curses by telling the truth, the whole truth, and nothing but the truth. As I continue to write the book and travel the world to share the story with others, I found that I too, like mom was healing from telling the story again and again and again.

My sister started working on loving herself. Craig ended his relationship in divorce. Oliviodale struggled with alcohol addiction but stayed close to his children.

I began my journey in acting. I stayed near water, after all that's where I found my peace. I continued my walks on the rivers and oceans. I did as my mother taught me. I set standards and morals that even I felt guilty and convicted if I compromised. I respected myself and made others respect me.

I learned during my journey of avoiding traps; I had to stick to my morals, set standards and understand stages we can all go through. I knew I had to leave Memphis to find the break I was looking for. It was a bitter sweet decision. However, I remembered mom telling me that she and dad came to Memphis to find a better way to live but never found it. She said instead she found trouble and a lifestyle of mediocrity. She said her dreams of living a lifestyle beyond mediocrity never came true. I too wanted to make it happen here in my hometown because I didn't want to uproot my business and move to Los Angeles or New York. I began to travel their intensively to take classes and search ways to better my acting career but it was something about home that made me stay. After living single for a while, I married the man that was a lot like my father – handsome, honest, godly, provider, quiet, introverted and respectful.

I was serious about my career in acting and appreciated everyone's advice. I decided to go to New York an audition for Acting Classes at Lee Strasberg School of Acting in Manhattan. Flashing back, I remember, I went in, met with a counselor and did my audition. I returned to Memphis not knowing if I had been accepted or not. The following week I received a call from the counselor. She told me I had been accepted and that classes were starting that Monday. In November of 2002, I packed my bags and went to register. I enrolled for 18 months.

I was called to the school on very short notice and didn't have time to give it much thought. I received a call on Thursday to report to school in New York City on Monday. When I arrived, I learned that the hotels were expensive in Manhattan. I remained in Manhattan, but found less expensive accommodations. I did little sleeping and lots of studying and meditating. The room reminded me of a rooming house with old furniture and shared bathrooms. It was frightening at first getting to know my way around and staying in New York. At first, I would walk and speak to everybody that passed me, but I soon learned that people in New York were busy getting where they were going. I stopped speaking and started concentrating on getting where I was going.

It got lonely traveling to New York every week, but I had committed to complete the 18-month curriculum. Every Monday morning, I caught the plane to New York for classes.

I called mom one night and shared with her how hard it was staying in New York. She wouldn't let me have self-pity instead she began to tell me that it was important to stay focused. She said, "The girls have their father taking care of them, you live in a two-story house, and you've got your sister and my support with your business." She went on to say, "Go to school and don't worry about your room." She said, "Concentrate on your education." I relaxed and stopped looking at the bad and began to enjoy studying in New York City.

I remembered being on the train one night going to my room, and noticed that the numbers were getting larger. As I watched for the Grand Central Station stop, I saw that the next stop was Harlem. I had been told how dangerous Harlem was and mom told me if I was going to go I needed to go with someone and during the day. I was both nervous and scared. I pulled my cell phone out, and called mom. The phone kept ringing; I was praying to God that she answered. Right, when I was about to hang up she said, "Hello" in her sleepy voice. I said, "Mom I'm in Harlem." Mom said, "Girl with who?" I told her I had gotten on the wrong train and the next stop was Harlem. She said, "Girl get back on the train and go in the opposite direction." She went on to say, "Didn't I tell you to never go to Harlem at night alone." I told her it was by mistake. Mom talked to me until I got on the train going back towards Manhattan.

Mom was back to that peachy color, beautiful smile mother I remembered. I was so excited she answered the phone. She stayed on the telephone until I got back to my room. We were laughing about the old comforter and raggedy black and white television in my room. Mom said I bet you can't wait to get back to that raggedy room, can you? I said Mom you're so right. I forgot all about how raggedy the room was. From that night forward, I did like mom said I concentrated on my acting classes, sense memories, voice, and singing. My instructors taught us that a great actor/actress was one that had a storage unit full of memories in which they could pull from. He told us the more disgusting memories we could remember, the more helpful the techniques would be while trying to bring a character to reality. I told him I had plenty in my storage. He said, they may not be bad after all. He said those might be the very memories that help me become a great actress.

I was grateful for the people that shared advice with me along the way. It was guidance that I needed. I met a Producer while in New York City, he was helpful connecting me to people, and the resources I needed to perfect my gift as an actress. I flew to Miami for an audition. I got the role. I loved being in Florida because I was drawn to water. However, there wasn't much work for me, so I went back to New York and finished my education.

I always believed that Hollywood was wherever the cameras were. I had acquired agents in Nashville, Miami, and Los Angeles. I didn't get many calls from them, because I wouldn't move from Memphis. I did land a few roles. My first part was in a movie called a "Family Thang" where I played a businesswoman. You didn't see much of me, only as I passed the leading character, Robert Duvall, in a courtroom scene. Later, I was called back by the same casting agency to film in "People vs. Larry Flynt". I was offered the part to play a madam; I see what my instructor meant by having memories in my storage because I did a good job bringing that character to life. All I had to do is think about mom and her friends they were running wild in her early days. I traveled to California later to finish filming. I was given the opportunity to film with the leading character Woody Harrelson and Courtney Love. Woody Harrelson asked, "Do you want to make some quick cash?" I answered. I was instructed by the producer to oblige the words, but after several takes, I took the risk of speaking. The director allowed the words to remain in the script, giving me the opportunity to become a S.A.G. Actress. My limo driver was very excited. He told me that was an opportunity that most directors didn't allow. I received a little more money and became S.A.G. eligible.

As I continued to prepare myself for opportunities, many cameras rolled into Memphis to film motion pictures. In 2004, the same producer that gave me the advice to move to Los Angeles back in 1993, returned to Memphis to film a movie titled "Hustle and Flow", my fans were excited. I was hoping that preparation was about to meet opportunity. I was praying that he had the discernment to know that I needed a break. I asked the Mayor of Memphis, to write me a letter of recommendation on my behalf, as a professional business owner of 18 years at the time and a S.A.G. Actress for 10 years. He wrote a beautiful letter of recommendation. The producer remembered our first meeting in 1993 and tried to give me the opportunity, but again, there were no speaking lines available, and I was given a cameo shot. It was disappointing and discouraging, but I took what I was offered. After all, I remembered how to appreciate what I was given. I flashed back thinking about when we stayed with auntie, she didn't have much food to give, but the little food she gave I appreciated it. So, though the role wasn't as much as I wanted it to be, I appreciated it. I threw a thank you party for my Mayor and a celebration for the cast and those fans for their support.

As I sat on the set somewhat disappointed that they were unable to give me speaking lines, the producer came around the corner. He was moving fast trying to get to the set, but I stopped him and reacquainted myself with him - he said oh yes, hi Sharon, it made me feel good that he knew my name. I told him the part had been cut as a news anchor, and as we stood on West Street off Crump Avenue in a low-income black neighborhood, around from one of the corners that we used to live as children, he said you're too sophisticated to play a role in this part. I said though because my education, entrepreneurship, accounting experience, and my licenses as a therapist and S.A.G. Actress had acquired me a bit of sophistication, the scene was being shot one street over, that held so many ugly childhood memories for me and represented a time of hustle for my mother not flowing back in the 70's. If anybody could have played a role in that film, it could have been me. I lived in that hood. The story was real for me.

I was near finishing my first year at The Lee Strasburg School, commuting weekly was getting tiresome, I looked for any excuse to stop going. I called mom told her I was tired and ready to give up on my career as an actress, it was taking long. Mom said, "You can't give up." She said, I was the only one that could stop my success by giving up. Mom's voice was slurred, it was late, and she was sleepy. She said keep the faith and do it for me, but most of all - do it for you.

I got up the next morning, attended my class and afterwards I caught the express bus to get to the airport. I was on my way home for the weekend. While I was riding the bus, my telephone rung, it was my sister from my shop, Ritzee Florist. I answered the call; she told me that she found mom in the bathroom of her apartment on the floor in a diabetic coma and that I needed to hurry home. I was frightened as the bus approached the Airport, I jumped off and rushed to catch the plane. When I arrived in Memphis, I rushed to the hospital. There laid my mother in a coma. This had happened once before, and she made it through, so I knew she would make it again. I got home from the hospital late that night, walked into my two-story house, greeted my husband with tears in my eyes and went upstairs to my girl's luxury rooms and kissed them on their foreheads. They asked is grandmother okay? I shook my head yes and said she's fine but let's pray. We prayed.

I was happy to look at my surroundings and witness the peace and beauty. I went back downstairs my husband was sitting quietly in our bedroom. He was in a state of meditation and our son was away. I was proud to have married a man like my father, a great provider, a man that loves God, an awesome father, a loving uncle and a man that helps children, unfortunate people, elders and the disabled. I took my shower and went straight to bed. Our girls came downstairs and quietly approached me and reminded me how much they loved me. I kiss them, hugged my husband and said good night. I crawled in our bed and held on to my pillow.

The telephone rang - it was a call from the doctor at the hospital. He stated that our mother had taken a turn for the worse and that we all needed to rush to the hospital as soon as possible. I called my two brothers, sister and all the grandchildren and we all rushed to the hospital. We prayed while mom laid there still unconscious. I looked at my mother as she lied in that hospital bed and I said to her, mom you can't leave me now - I need you. I saw a tear drop from her eyes and I felt her spirit say to me, "Do it for me, but most of all do it for you". I knew then that I couldn't give up, I had to make this acting career a success. I knew within my heart I could never give up on my acting career and I then became more determined than ever to get a break. The doctor came in and said that all her vital signs were shutting down and that this was abnormal, because she was doing great yesterday. Then he asked, if we take her off the machine and she doesn't breathe on her own, did we want him to resuscitate her?

Jackie, Craig, Oliviodale and I asked for a moment alone. The doctor left the room as we contemplated on what to do. We all stood over mom, and considered what her eyes were saying and shared our moments with her. I wished she told Oliviodale he didn't have to go through what she had gone through in her life by self-medicating his pain with excessive drinking and drugging. I prayed she told him that she wanted him to be successful and to supersede her life. Mom often got angry with Oliviodale when he would excessively drink or take downers, because she knew the damage it had done to her. As my oldest brother considered her eyes, I hoped she told him to raise his children, but don't let women abuse him. I prayed she told him don't live a lie but take control in his household and don't keep the truth from his children. I prayed she told my oldest sister that for all the times she had given up her childhood to help her raise us, she was going to receive great rewards and that her day was going to come that she would have peace and the things her heart desired. I prayed that she apologized to her and told her how much she loved her and how she really regretted the things she had put her through as a child. However, honestly all I know is what mom told me. I looked at my mother and searched deeply for what she had to say to me. She just looked at me with tears in her eyes and said tell the truth Sharon, the whole truth, and nothing but the truth, and she said, "Jesus died for you first, and I died for you second." She reminded me not to abuse my body with drugs and alcohol, not to ever leave my husband, and to give my girls and son quality time and do all I could to bond with my sister. She said I expect you to succeed in your acting career. I took on the responsibility, to tell the truth, the whole truth and nothing but the truth. As the children walked out of the room to decide, the grandchildren went into the room. I prayed again and hoped that she told them she never meant to make a difference and that she loved them all the same. I prayed she told them she cursed the spirit in them that reminded her of any of the devastating things she had experienced. I knew she didn't want to see them make the same mistakes she made in life, and for those that weren't there, I knew she would have wanted them to know she loved them all the same and to never compete for love and attention. As my siblings and I walked back into the room, we looked at each other and then considered mom's eyes, and we asked her if she was ready to cross over? There was an expression that came over her face, and we knew that she was ready.

Mom waited for everyone to get to the hospital. We all kissed her, and when her sister arrived, the doctor came back into the room, turned the machine off and mom took one breath and crossed over - she didn't come back to us that morning. Mom died. We all left sad and some crying.

I recall telling mom I wanted any excuse to stop going to New York to attend school, but I turned that around, mom became my motivation to return. The next week I got on the plane and headed to New York. Once the plane landed, I got off the plane walked into my raggedy room, put my bags down and took it all in. I sat for a moment and meditated. I could hear mom saying, "Sharon tell the truth, the whole truth and nothing but the truth." Mom started coming to me in my dreams, and at other times she would come when I was near water or even if it rained. I realized I had generational curses and demonic strongholds that I had to pull down and break. I began to travel more to write mom's story. It was something about being near water that gave me the peace I needed to re-live those childhood memories openly. I soon realized it was the faith that I had; knowing I would feel mom's spirit at the water.

Telling the truth was like turning the light on roaches. Everybody scattered, but we all came back together. I realized that it was mom's rags that kept me from falling into the devastating traps life had set for me. I had no one to blame. I was happy to make it through and became aware that these were curses that had been suppressed and never dealt with.

Mom's story began to help heal my family. I learned that my material wealth, businesses, good jobs, fine cars, two and three-story homes, penthouses, mansions and fine clothes had very little to do with my material riches but a lot to do with my mother's rags and faith in the power of prayer. Our mom's struggles in life helped me to avoid the traps of so many abusive behaviors and bad habits. I sure do thank that mean old great-grandmother for beating that very thing in me that she beat in mom, which was God. To this day I trust that force, that spiritual force of God and the force of my mother's spirit.

I wondered how mom could write through me. While I wrote her story, I kept in mind of what she said. I was happy to see the rain come, because I knew I would be writing and I knew mom spirit would be present. She always said go to the water, and I will meet you there. I learned to trust her spirit.

Now that all the ugly memories were out I could get back to those special moments we shared. I could smile when I thought about those long talks mom, and I had. I could smell those awesome dinners she cooked for us. When the holidays came around, I no longer cried, but instead, I remembered those apples and peppermint sticks mom put out. It was great to think on all the good things we experienced. Getting pass all those bad memories allowed the fun memories to return. I was glad to know that mom had that opportunity to talk to God before dying. I sure do appreciate that peachy colored skin, Coca-Cola bottle shaped woman with that beautiful smile and wavy hair. She really taught us how not to live, and I thank her for the life she lived. I was blessed to graduate, publish mom's book and use it to help little children and mother's like those we saw at the beginning of the story. The W in the rags stood for what rags had been hidden in our family that caused so much pain. The t in the riches was a symbol, a cross that reminded me that prayer works. I surely needed it to face the truth. It is my hope that our story will help to heal the land just like it helped me heal and to recreate myself. Mom and Dad, I love you.

The End

CPSIA information can be obtained
at www.ICGtesting.com
Printed in the USA
LVHW08s0138100818
586431LV00001B/24/P